Shine!

The Horatio Alger Musical

Book by
Richard Seff
Music by
Roger Dean Anderson
Lyrics by
Lee Goldsmith

A SAMUEL FRENCH ACTING EDITION

NEW YORK HOLLYWOOD LONDON TORONTO

SAMUELFRENCH.COM

Book Copyright © 2001, 2002, 2011 by Richard Seff
Lyrics Copyright © 2001, 2002, 2011 by Lee Goldsmith

ALL RIGHTS RESERVED

Cover photo credit: Steven Rosen
Used by permission
Actor pictured: Andy Mientus

CAUTION: Professionals and amateurs are hereby warned that *SHINE! THE HORATIO ALGER MUSICAL* is subject to a licensing fee. It is fully protected under the copyright laws of the United States of America, the British Commonwealth, including Canada, and all other countries of the Copyright Union. All rights, including professional, amateur, motion picture, recitation, lecturing, public reading, radio broadcasting, television and the rights of translation into foreign languages are strictly reserved. In its present form the play is dedicated to the reading public only.

The amateur and professional live stage performance rights to *SHINE! THE HORATIO ALGER MUSICAL* are controlled exclusively by Samuel French, Inc., and licensing arrangements and performance licenses must be secured well in advance of presentation. PLEASE NOTE that amateur licensing fees are set upon application in accordance with your producing circumstances. When applying for a licensing quotation and a performance license please give us the number of performances intended, dates of production, your seating capacity and admission fee. Licensing fees are payable one week before the opening performance of the play to Samuel French, Inc., at 45 W. 25th Street, New York, NY 10010.

Licensing fee of the required amount must be paid whether the play is presented for charity or gain and whether or not admission is charged.

Professional/Stock licensing fees quoted upon application to Samuel French, Inc.

For all other rights than those stipulated above, apply to: Samuel French, Inc., at 45 W. 25th Street, New York, NY 10010.

Particular emphasis is laid on the question of amateur or professional readings, permission and terms for which must be secured in writing from Samuel French, Inc.

Copying from this book in whole or in part is strictly forbidden by law, and the right of performance is not transferable.

Whenever the play is produced the following notice must appear on all programs, printing and advertising for the play: "Produced by special arrangement with Samuel French, Inc."

Due authorship credit must be given on all programs, printing and advertising for the play.

ISBN 978-0-573-62928-0   Printed in U.S.A.   #21529

No one shall commit or authorize any act or omission by which the copyright of, or the right to copyright, this play may be impaired.

No one shall make any changes in this play for the purpose of production.

Publication of this play does not imply availability for performance. Both amateurs and professionals considering a production are strongly advised in their own interests to apply to Samuel French, Inc., for written permission before starting rehearsals, advertising, or booking a theatre.

No part of this book may be reproduced, stored in a retrieval system, or transmitted in any form, by any means, now known or yet to be invented, including mechanical, electronic, photocopying, recording, videotaping, or otherwise, without the prior written permission of the publisher.

RENTAL MATERIALS

An orchestration consisting of a **Piano/Conductor's Score, Chorus Books, Piano 1, Piano 2, Violin, Cello, and Various percussion, to be shared by all musicians** will be loaned two months prior to the production ONLY on the receipt of the Licensing Fee quoted for all performances, the rental fee and a refundable deposit.

Please contact Samuel French for perusal of the music materials as well as a performance license application.

IMPORTANT BILLING AND CREDIT REQUIREMENTS

All producers of *SHINE! THE HORATIO ALGER MUSICAL must* give credit to the Authors of the Play in all programs distributed in connection with performances of the Play, and in all instances in which the title of the Play appears for the purposes of advertising, publicizing or otherwise exploiting the Play and/or a production. The name of the Authors *must* appear on a separate line on which no other name appears, immediately following the title and must appear in size of type not less than fifty percent of the size of the title type. Greg Anthony as Orchestrator/Co-Arranger shall receive credit wherever and whenever more than two (2) members of the creative team (excluding the authors and stars) shall receive credit. Such credit shall appear in the same size and boldness as that accorded to any other member of the creative team other than the director and any stars.

In addition the following credit *must* be given in all programs and publicity information distributed in association with this piece:

(NAME OF PRODUCER)

Presents

SHINE!
The Horatio Alger Musical

Book by **RICHARD SEFF**

Music by **ROGER DEAN ANDERSON**

Lyrics by **LEE GOLDSMITH**

Originally presented in New York City in the 2010
New York Musical Theatre Festival
Isaac Robert Hurwitz, Executive Director & Producer

In association with
Other Side Productions
Peter Mercurio, Artistic Director

The World Premiere of the revised edition of *SHINE! THE HORATIO ALGER MUSICAL* was part of the 2010 New York Musical Theatre Festival, presented in association with Other Side Productions at Theater at St. Clement's in New York City. The performance was directed by Peter Flynn, with choreography by Devanand Janki, music direction by Annbritt duChateau, orchestrations by Greg Anthony, set and costume designs by Michael Bottari and Ron Case, and lighting by Jeff Croiter. The cast was as follows:

RICHARD HUNTER ("RAGGED DICK")	Andy Mientus
LUKE GERRISH	Michael Halling
STACIA JANE HAUSER	Meggie Cansler
SILAS SNOBDEN	William Ryall
GIDEON CHAPIN	Jimmy Ray Bennett
HIGGINS	Stanton Nash
ALLEN CARLISLE	Philip Chaffin
ROB CARLISLE	Tyler Merna
FOSWELL	Dan Lawler
MRS. MOONEY	Katherine McGrath
MRS. McHUGH	Joy Hermalyn
MICKEY McGUIRE	Evan Jay Newman
VENDOR'S CUSTOMER, ENSEMBLE	Melissa Rain Anderson
BUSINESS MAN, ENSEMBLE	Cheo Bourne
MRS. HALLIWELL, ENSEMBLE	Rachel Coloff
CRONY, ENSEMBLE	Todd Horman
CRONY, ENSEMBLE	Jason Mills
BUSINESS MAN, ENSEMBLE	Robert Mintz
VENDOR, ENSEMBLE	Jessica Vosk

CHARACTERS

(in order of appearance)

3 BUSINESSMEN (ensemble roles)

A STREET VENDOR (ensemble role)

OFFICER FOY – a Policeman (ensemble role)

RICHARD HUNTER – ("Ragged Dick") Age: 16-18. Brash and confident with much charm. Must be exceptional singer-actor.

MICKEY McGUIRE – Age: 15-19. A street tough. Clever, selfish, a wise-guy.

HENRY FOSWELL – Age: 15-17. Hunter's friend and opposite. Bookish and intelligent, but with no street smarts.

GIDEON CHAPIN – Age: 40s. Uptight and mean-spirited clerk in charge at Snobden's store. Conniving and unpleasant. A comic villain.

ALLEN CARLISLE – Age: early 40s. Handsome, likable. A diamond in the rough; very wealthy now, was once poor.

HERBERT HIGGINS – Age: 20s-30s. Ambitious but weak underling to Chapin. Slightly hysterical at times. Actor should be up to low comedy.

SILAS SNOBDEN – Age: 50s-60s. Proprietor of Snobden, Inc. a haberdashery. Precise and demanding, but fair and not unkind. Could be plump, bald or both. Needs good character singing voice.

LUKE GERRISH – Age: late 30s, early 40s. Amoral, cynical, cunning and dangerous. Attractive to women and knows it. Baritone.

TWO CRONIES – male acquaintances of Luke Gerrish. (ensemble roles)

STACIA-JANE HAUSER – Age: late 20s-early 30s. Attractive, but not necessarily beautiful. Working class background. Intelligent though not well educated. Soprano or chest.

MARY McHUGH – Age: 50s. Irish landlady. Addled, disheveled, ditzy. We like her. Sings in a beery way. (Ensemble role)

FINOLA MAY MOONEY – Age: late 40s or 50s. Hearty, good-natured, shrewd. And very Irish.

ROB CARLISLE – Age: 8. Carlisle's son. Bright and self confident, not a brat.

MRS. O'MALLEY, MRS. CASSIDY, MRS. O'LEARY – neighborhood women, Friends of Mrs. Mooney. (Ensemble roles)

MRS. HALLIWELL – Stylish woman of 40, oozes charm, is a bit of a snob. (Ensemble role)

MALE ENSEMBLE – Man #1, Man #2, Man #3, Man #4

FEMALE ENSEMBLE – Woman #1, Woman #2, Woman #3, Woman #4

ABOUT THE SHOW

SHINE! is an original musical comedy based on characters and situations found in the works of Horatio Alger, particularly *Ragged Dick* and *Silas Snobden's Office Boy*, respectively Alger's first bestseller and the one first printed in book form eighty years after it was serialized in *Argosy*. We've borrowed characters from both novels, youthened some, aged others, reinvented a few, created a few of our own. And of course we gave them songs to sing and comic devices Horatio did not provide. But we stuck with Alger's pervasive theme: that in America one could begin with nothing, and with the right attitude, hard work, application, and a little bit of luck, dream a dream and chart a course on which to achieve it. The road was rutted, it twisted and turned, it was loaded with chance encounters and bothersome detours, but if one got on with it, didn't complain about the rough days and the tragic losses, well - it could lead all who traveled it right smack into a musical comedy.

Welcome to the world of *SHINE!* It probably will not make you rich. It may not even get you started up the road to success. On the other hand, it may -

–*Richard Seff*

MUSICAL NUMBERS
ACT ONE

Scene 1: Wall Street, a morning in April 1876
"The Good Old Days" ....COMPANY
"Shine" .... **DICK, MICKEY, FOSWELL**, and **BUSINESS MEN**
"Respectable" .... **DICK**

Scene 2: Snobden's Haberdashery Shop
"Silas Snobden, Inc." .... **CHAPIN, HIGGINS, SNOBDEN, DICK**

Scene 3: Street Outside Snobden's
"Cock and Bull" .... LUKE

Scene 4: Outside Mrs. McHugh's Boarding House, late afternoon same day
"Maybe Today" .... STACIA

Scene 5: Front of the Wall St. Saloon, that evening

Scene 6: The Wall St. Saloon
"Put Your Money In" .... THE WALL ST. BUCKS, DICK, FOSWELL

Scene 7: Mrs. Mooney's Stoop
"The Room" .... MRS. MOONEY
"Respectable" (reprise) .... DICK

Scene 8: A Street Near Carlisle's Bank
"Keeping Up With The Times" .... SNOBDEN, DICK, FOSWELL, CARLISLE, HIGGINS, COMPANY

Scene 9: Stacia's Room at Mrs. McHugh's, an evening in late June
"Maybe Today (reprise)" .... STACIA

Scene 10: A Street in Lower Manhattan, another day in June

Scene 11: Snobden's Store, morning in early July
"A Hardworking Boy" .... CHAPIN, HIGGINS
"Look How Far We've Come" .... CARLISLE

Scene 12: Union Square, July 4th 1876
"Look How Far We've Come" (cont'd) .... CARLISLE, DICK, MRS.MOONEY, MRS. McHUGH, FOSWELL, COMPANY

ACT TWO

Scene 1: A Street in Wall St. Area, later that day
"Find That Boy!" .... DICK, CARLISLE, COMPANY

Scene 2: Snobden's Store, two days later, very early morning
"A Hardworking Boy" (reprise) .... CHAPIN, HIGGINS
"Shine" (reprise) .... DICK

Scene 3: Stacia's Room, later the same day
"From Now On" .... LUKE, STACIA
"Maybe Today" (reprise) .... STACIA

Scene 4: Wall Street Area
"Yes!" .... DICK

Scene 5: Stoop in front of Mrs. Mooney's, later that evening
"A Handful O' Hops" .... MRS. MOONEY, MRS. McHUGH, MRS. O'MALLEY, MRS. CASSIDY, MRS. O'LEARY, DICK, FOSWELL

Scene 6: Stacia's Room

Scene 7: On the trolley, the next day

Scene 8: Various locations, heading uptown, Saturday Night
"North of 14th Street" .... COMPANY

*To my mother
Henrietta
who started it all.*

ACT I

(SETTING: A show curtain or backdrop, painted in the style of productions of the Old Bowery Theater, featuring an unfinished Brooklyn Bridge and the skyline of New York City, circa 1876. Displayed prominently are the words: "WALL STREET IS KING AND VIRTUE IS ITS OWN REWARD.")

(TIME: Seven o'clock, a morning in late April, 1876.)

(AT RISE: Our **ENTIRE CAST** *in tableaux: Among them, a street vendor, a policeman, a wealthy woman, a poor one, a lower class man and young woman, hand in hand, well-dressed gents and middle class gents. The sounds of church bells and carriages; a musical vamp of metallic klangs and wooden klops brings them all to sudden vocal and busy life. A young newsboy announces headlines ["Extra!" etc.], 2 men buy from him.* **MICKEY** *steals one of the papers. He sells it to a third* **MAN***, who pays with a bill.* **MAN** *reads headline, waits for change, his hand out – turns –* **MICKEY** *is gone. The policeman follows after him. On cue, the 3 newspapers flip open, one by one, like Chinese fans. The men sing:)*

Song - *THE GOOD OLD DAYS*

MAN #1.

RISING CRIME RATES!

MAN #2.

HIGHER PRICES!

BOTH.

WHAT HAS BECOME
OF THE GOOD OLD DAYS?

MAN #3.

NOW NEW YORK IS
DIRT AND VICES –

ALL 3.
>CAN'T WE HAVE SOME
>OF THE GOOD OLD DAYS?
>
>*(The **CAST** whistles as the morning activity continues: casual greetings and curious crossings by characters who will connect later in the play, the vendor setting up wares, the policeman still following **MICKEY**, etc.)*

OFFICER FOY (MAN #4).
>I REMEMBER
>HOW IT BECKONED,
>LITTLE NEW YORK

ALL.
>IN THE GOOD OLD DAYS –

WOMAN #1.
>NOW IT'S NORTH OF
>FORTY-SECOND –

ALL.
>POPPING ITS CORK
>SINCE THE GOOD OLD DAYS!

MAN #1. *(towards the direction of the bridge)*
>OVER TO BROOKLYN
>THEY'RE RAISING UP THAT MONSTER

ALL. *(all eyes following upward)*
>OF A GREAT BIG BRIDGE!

MAN #2.
>WATCH IT ALL FALL DOWN!

MAN #3.
>IF GOD WANTED BRIDGES
>THEN WHY WOULD HE PROVIDE US WITH THAT
>BRAND NEW FLEET OF FERRIES?

WOMAN #2. *(pointing in the other direction)*
>OUT IN THE HARBOR,
>THEY'RE PLANNING SOME COLOSSUS –

ALL. *(turning)*
>IT'S A DAMN FOOL THING!

WOMAN #1.
>WHAT A WASTE OF CASH!

WOMAN #3.

>DESIGNED BY A FRENCHMAN,
>SOME USELESS, SILLY STATUE JUST TO
>WELCOME ALL THAT
>FOREIGN RIFF-RAFF –

WOMEN.

>SINCE THEY GOT HERE
>HOW THINGS HAVE CHANGED
>FROM THE GOOD OLD DAYS!

MEN.

>THOUGH WE MIGHT WISH
>THEY WERE NOT HERE,

ALL. *(unison)*

>WE'VE REARRANGED
>FROM THE GOOD OLD DAYS!
>NOW ALL TOGETHER
>WE'RE WASTING TIME WHILE WATCHING ALL
>THOSE BASEBALL GAMES!

WOMEN.

>WHAT A STUPID SPORT!

MEN.

>PERHAPS WE SHOULD READ MORE
>OR FANCY ALL THE FINER THINGS

ALL. *(gradually)*

>LIKE LONG, LONG GERMAN OPERAS?

>*(The **CROWD** frantically moves into a cluster as if now being tossed about on an elevated train in motion. An **IRISH CLEANING LADY**, working away on her knees, is forced aside in the rush.)*

CLEANING LADY (WOMAN #4).

>ELEVATED!
>SPITTIN' CINDERS –
>HORSES WERE BEST
>IN THE GOOD OLD DAYS.
>
>STRANGERS RIDIN'
>PAST ME WINDERS—
>HOW WE WERE BLESSED
>IN THE GOOD OLD DAYS!

EVERYONE ELSE. *(gradually)*
> GODLESS BRIDGES,
> STATUES IN THE HARBOR,
> RIFF-RAFF!
> BASEBALL!
>
> *(adding* **CLEANING LADY***)*
>
> EL-E-VATED!

ALL.
> EVEN SO WE
> LOVE THIS CITY!
> THEY WERE ASLEEP
> IN THE GOOD OLD DAYS –
>
> 'CROSS THE HUDSON
> LIFE'S A PITY!
> THERE THEY CAN KEEP
> ALL THEIR GOOD OLD DAYS!

(The vamp continues, simplifies. The **POLICEMAN** *[***OFFICER FOY***], whistling, approaches a wooden crate that is now clearly visible. Taps on the side with his baton.)*

(A **YOUNG MAN** *in his late teens,* **RICHARD HUNTER***, in ragged clothes and covered in some straw, suddenly pokes his head up from the box.)*

OFFICER FOY. Well now, Dick. This isn't the Astor House. We don't sleep till noon in this hotel.

DICK. *(half-asleep)* What time is it?

FOY. Seven o'clock.

(Through the following **DICK** *runs his fingers through his hair, picking the straw from it. He puts on his jacket which has been his pillow and uncovers a shoeshine box hidden in the straw.)*

DICK. Seven o'clock! I oughter been up an hour ago. Kind of you to wake me, Officer Foy.

FOY. A little service from the city.

DICK. Treated myself to a fine theatrical at the Old Bowery and didn't turn in till past midnight.

FOY. You went to the Old Bowery?

DICK. It was so grand. Heroes, villains, lots of daring-do and no lack of pretty girls.

FOY. And how did you get the money for such an extravaganza?

DICK. Boot blackin' and shoeshines, of course.

FOY. Stick to it till you get something better.

DICK. I mean to, but it ain't easy to get out of, as the prisoner said about his residence.

FOY. I hope you don't speak from experience.

DICK. You won't catch me stealin', if that's what you mean.

FOY. I know that.

(FOY tosses DICK the uneaten apple as he exits, whistling. DICK catches it, gives it a quick shine before taking a bite. He begins to shine his own shoes. MICKEY MAGUIRE enters, still avoiding OFFICER FOY, plain shoebox in hand, smoking a cigar.)

MICKEY. Hey, Dick. We missed you at poker last night.

DICK. Yeah? How much did you lose this time?

(a pause, obviously a lot)

MICKEY. Who spilled the beans?

DICK. I can't transact no loans, Mick. I started late today. Missed my regulars.

MICKEY. Just enough to buy your less fortunate friend some breakfast?

(DICK takes MAGUIRE's cigar, puffs on it.)

DICK. You should try workin' for your money sometime. This rag of mine is gonna blacken a lot of boots today. Now get outta here before I blacken your right eye.

MICKEY. Oh, Dick, you are so good! I bet you don't know why you ain't in heaven right now instead of bein' down here with us lowlifes.

(MICKEY takes back the cigar. Just then, a boy, HENRY FOSWELL, enters. He is younger than DICK or MICKEY.

He stands there, not knowing what to do or where to go. He holds a shoeshine box.)

MICKEY. *(to* **DICK***)* Who's that?

DICK. Never seen him before.

MICKEY. Hey, kid. Get outta here. This is our territory.

DICK. Leave him be. *(to* **FOSWELL***)* Are you lost?

FOSWELL. I don't think so. *(He notices the boot boxes.)* So you're both bootblacks?

DICK. I am. Professional. He's just foolin' around.

MICKEY. Oh yes, this here is his Majesty, King of the Bootblacks.

FOSWELL. Then maybe you can help me. I've never done this before.

MICKEY. Sure, kid – We'll give you some pointers.

(They circle the **BOY***, sizing him up.)*

FOSWELL. *(to* **DICK***)* Those clothes are kind of funny. Is that a costume?

DICK. I'll have you know these pants was worn by Napoleon at the Battle of Waterloo! He was short so they're small on me.

MICKEY. Aw, Dick – save it for the customers.

DICK. *(ignoring him)* What I'm telling you kid is you gotta have a story. And take your time with a customer. They gotta feel they're getting' somethin'. And what they're getting' is quality and that means tips. Now, look.

(He takes **FOSWELL***'s shoe.)*

You can't brush too hard, you'll just scruff the shoe up worse. But you can't brush too soft, or what's the point? See here? That's beautiful, ain't it?

*(***MICKEY** *spins* **FOSWELL** *around.)*

MICKEY. Look, it's like this, kid. You gotta eat, right? And you don't have money to throw away so watch this. You got your rag and you got your tin of polish. And take a little tin of water. Water's free. The polish'll cost you.

*(He demonstrates on **FOSWELL**'s other shoe.)*

MICKEY. *(cont.)* So you take your rag and dip it into the water. If you run out, use your spit. Then you run it around the polish, just so the rag looks black, and you shine 'em up. Now look at that. By the time their shoes dry, they'll be long outta sight, outta mind.

DICK. Right. And you'll never see them again, whereas they coulda become a regular. For instance.

*(A **BUSINESSMAN** crosses. **DICK** springs into action.)*

Shine your shoes, sir?

CUSTOMER (MAN #1). No time, son. I have important business at City Hall.

DICK. Be sure to give my regards to the Mayor. Just tell him Ragged Dick. He'll know.

CUSTOMER (MAN #1). *(still on his way, stops)* Friend of yours, is he?

DICK. I black his boots by special appointment. That's how I pay my city taxes. His honor wouldn't consider going to the City Hall without a shine from yours truly.

CUSTOMER (MAN #1). And why is that?

Song - SHINE

DICK.

HERE'S A BOX
WHERE YOU WOULD NEVER GUESS
THERE IS MAGIC LURKING –

IT UNLOCKS
THE SECRET OF SUCCESS –
AND I GUARANTEE IT WON'T STOP WORKING!

CUSTOMER (MAN #1). Maybe tomorrow.

DICK.

IT MAY BE JUST A SHOESHINE
BUT I AM HERE TO SAY
THAT WHEN YOU'VE GOT A NEW SHINE
YOU'RE WELL ON YOUR WAY!

DICK.
> TO KEEP YOUR DAY FROM LACKIN'
> IN OPPORTUNITY –
> JUST TRY A BIT OF BLACKIN'
> PROVIDED BY ME!

*(**FOSWELL** is watching closely, and has taken out a pencil and small pad. He is writing notes. **MICKEY** watches, bored, chewing on his cigar, while attempting to steal an apple from the vendor cart.)*

CUSTOMER. Very well, then.

DICK.
> A SHINE
> IS REALLY ALL THAT YOU NEED
> AND YOU WILL SEE
> THERE'LL BE
> A CHANGE IN YOUR LUCK!
>
> A SHINE
> AND YOU ARE BOUND TO SUCCEED
> AND BY TONIGHT
> YOU MIGHT
> BE J.P. MORGAN!

*(The **CUSTOMER** is amused by this. "Well, we'll see about that... etc.")*

> YOUR COAT IS THIN AND THREADBARE,
> YOUR PANTS ARE WORSE THAN THAT –
> YOU HAVE TO KEEP YOUR HEAD BARE
> CAUSE YOU'VE GOT NO HAT –
>
> BUT IF YOU'VE GOT ENDURANCE,
> YOU'RE GONNA DO JUST FINE –
> WITH FAITH AND SELF-ASSURANCE
> AND THE PRICE OF A SHINE!

*(He finishes with a flair. The **CUSTOMER** admires the job, grandly pays with a coin and rushes off. **DICK** shines the nickel, pockets it and returns to **FOSWELL**.)*

DICK. See? It's not so tough. *(sees the pencil and pad)* What's that?

FOSWELL. I like to take notes.

DICK. You're never gonna learn how to shine shoes by scribblin' on paper. You wanna be an artist you gotta create. Tell you what I'll do. If you're up to it, I'll get us each a customer.

FOSWELL. Can you do that?!

DICK. Can do. Mickey, you feel like shockin' us and doin' some work for a change?

MICKEY. Sure. I'll try anything once.

DICK. Watch.

(**DICK** *spies* **3 BUSINESSMEN**.)

FIRST MAN (MAN #2). I'm telling you Ambrose, you'd better pick up some Erie Railroad Common. It's a bargain and it's goin' through the roof.

DICK. *(sidling up to them)* Excuse me, Gentlemen, but my associates and I were hoping you might help settle a business dispute we are having.

SECOND MAN (MAN #4). And what might that be?

DICK. My friend here, Mister…

(realizes he doesn't know Foswell's name)

FOSWELL. Foswell.

DICK. My friend, Mr. Foswell –

(**DICK** *does a double take on this.*)

Mister Foswell here insists that your boots haven't seen a shine for at least two days. But I say it's more like a week.

THIRD MAN (MAN #3). Well, son, you're both wrong. We had a shine not an hour ago before we made the crossing from Brooklyn.

DICK. Ah well, there you are. That explains it.

(The **BOYS** *nod in agreement.)*

FIRST MAN. Explains what?

DICK. The bootblacks in Brooklyn ain't up to our professional standards here in Manhattan.

THIRD MAN. Nonsense. A shine is a shine.

DICK. No, mister – With all due respect –

(DICK begins his pitch.)

SOME THINK THERE'S NOTHING TO IT –
JUST GIVE A RAG A TWIST –
BUT AMATEURS CAN'T DO IT –
THEY DON'T HAVE THE WRIST –

YOUR SHOES WON'T MIND THE WEATHER –
OUR SECRET KEEPS 'EM FIT

MICKEY.

YOU FURNISH US THE LEATHER,
WE'LL FURNISH THE SPIT!

(DICK uses MICKEY to illustrate his story, perhaps charming a carnation from the VENDOR as a bridal bouquet for MICKEY.)

DICK. *(continuing)*

LET'S SAY
YOU'VE FOUND THE GIRL YOU WOULD CHOOSE
TO BE YOUR WIFE
FOR LIFE
SO YOU SET THE DATE!

BUT HEY
SHE TAKES ONE LOOK AT YOUR SHOES

MICKEY. *(as the bride)*

AND LEAVES YOU FLAT –
LIKE THAT –

BOTH.

RIGHT AT THE ALTAR!

SECOND MAN. *(charmed, giving in)* All right, boys. Let's see what you can do.

(DICK, a reluctant MICKEY, and a comic, clumsy FOSWELL set up their boxes and proceed to shine the MEN's boots as "SHINE" and "GOOD OLD DAYS" merge in a contrapuntal chorus, reaching a climax with...)

3 BOYS.

    IT MAY BE JUST A SHOE SHINE
    BUT I AM HERE TO SAY
    THAT WHEN YOU'VE GOT A NEW SHINE
    YOU'RE WELL ON YOUR WAY!

    TO KEEP YOUR DAYS FROM LACKIN'
        IN OPPORTUNITY
    JUST TRY A BIT O' BLACKIN' PROVIDED
        BY ME!

    A SHINE
    IS REALLY ALL THAT YOU NEED
    AND YOU WILL SEE THERE'LL BE
    A CHANGE IN YOUR LUCK!

    A SHINE
    AND YOU ARE BOUND TO SUCCEED
    AND BY TONIGHT YOU MIGHT BE
    J.P. MORGAN!

3 BUSINESS MEN.

    WE REMEMBER
    HOW IT BECKONED,
    LITTLE NEW YORK
    IN THE GOOD OLD DAYS –

    NOW IT'S NORTH OF FORTY
        SECOND!
    POPPING IT'S CORK
    SINCE THE GOOD OLD DAYS –

    OVER TO BROOKLYN
    THEIR RAISING UP
    THAT GREAT BIG BRIDGE!

    (WHILE) OUT IN THE HARBOR
    THEY PLAN TO BUILD THIS
    DAMN, FOOL USELESS STATUE!

    BASEBALL AND RIFF-RAFF
    AND ELEVATED
    SPITTIN CINDERS!

ALL. *(in unison)*

    SO IF YOU WOULD DISCOVER
    THE SECRET OF YOUR GROWTH
    TO MILLIONAIRE OR LOVER
    OR PREF'RABLY BOTH!

    THE RULE COULD NOT BE STRICTER –
    IT'S THAT WAY BY DESIGN,
    THE FIGHT THAT ENDS IN VICTORY
    BEGINS WITH A SHINE!

DICK. *(solo)*

    RECALL THAT DECLARATION
    THE PROMISE TO OUR NATION

ALL.

    OF LIBERTY AND LIFE
    AND THE PURSUIT OF A SHINE!

*(When the number ends, **DICK**, **FOSWELL**, and **MICKEY** have finished their shines.)*

DICK'S CUSTOMER (MAN #3). *(admiring his shoes, and paying)* Excellent work. Five cents – that's what I call a bargain!

FOSWELL'S CUSTOMER (MAN #4). *(inspecting the job and giving him a nickel)* Not bad. Here's your nickel.

FOSWELL. "Not bad!" Did you hear? *(then to* **DICK***)* Thanks!

(**FOSWELL** *exits.*)

MICKEY'S CUSTOMER (MAN #2). They looked better in Brooklyn. Here's three cents. You won't see me again.

MICKEY. *(following the* **MAN** *offstage)* Oh yeah! Well, I'll just have to struggle along without'cha!

(**DICK** *spots another potential customer, hurriedly crossing.*)

DICK. Shine your shoes, sir?

MAN. *(later known as* **CHAPIN***)* Not now! I'm late.

DICK. Always time for a shine. Don't mind my saying, looks like you could use one.

MAN. How dare you hand out advice on grooming! Look at you! You're nothing but a guttersnipe.

(*He exits in a rush into a nearby shop, closing the door in* **DICK***'s face, as…*)

DICK. This coat once belonged to General George Washington! Oh yes! He wore it crossin' the Delaware!

(**ALLEN CARLISLE**, *an impressive looking gent, who has entered shortly after the* **MAN**, *has witnessed the above.*)

CARLISLE. *(to* **DICK***)* It seems you have distinguished friends. *(seriously)* You mustn't let him upset you.

DICK. These clothes? I only wear 'em cause they help folks to notice me.

CARLISLE. I once knew a boot-black who got just three cents a shine. You're getting five. You're already ahead of him.

(*He picks up* **DICK***'s polishing rag.*)

This cloth isn't bad. But if I wanted to make some extra money, I'd get a heavier one. It'll do a better job and in less time. Add some finesse.

DICK. Finesse. And that's good?

CARLISLE. "Finesse." French word I've borrowed. "Extreme delicacy or subtlety in action." I just heard it this morning and I wanted to try it out.

DICK. I do that! But I'm still workin' on English.

CARLISLE. Right. I was being a bit grand.

DICK. No, no! I'd give you a shine for the advice, but I don't think I could match the one you've got.

CARLISLE. Thank you. I do them myself.

DICK. You're better'n me. And I'm good.

CARLISLE. Maybe I missed a couple of spots. Why don't you take a crack at them?

DICK. Yes sir!

Song - *RESPECTABLE*

(glancing up at **CARLISLE***)*

HEY WILL YOU LOOK AT HIM –
I WONDER WHO HE IS –
THIS FELLA, PROUD AND TALL,
YOU'D THINK THAT ALL
THE WORLD IS HIS –

(He starts the shine.)

JUST TAKE A LOOK AT HIM –
IT'S CLEAR TO SEE
HE'S ALL THE THINGS I'M NOT
BUT KNOW I'VE GOT
THE CHANCE TO BE –

BUT IT'S SO VERY FAR
FROM BLACKIN' BOOTS
TO WEARIN' SILK CRAVATS
AND DERBY (TALL TOP) HATS
AND LINEN SUITS –

NO MATTER WHAT HE DOES –
NO MATTER WHO HE WAS –
WHEN PEOPLE LOOK HIS WAY
THEY SIMPLY SAY
"RESPECTABLE."

CARLISLE. *(quietly)* Do you live with your folks?

DICK. No folks. I'm on my own at The Box Hotel. *(beat)* But you wouldn't know about that.

CARLISLE. I might.

(He raises the paper and reads. **DICK** *continues the shine.)*

DICK.
> THOUGH SHINING SHOES REMAINS
> A WORTHY CHORE,
> AS EVERY DAY GOES BY
> I'VE GOT TO TRY
> AND REACH FOR MORE!
>
> I'M NOT A LIKELY LAD,
> I CAN'T COMPARE –
> AND IF I WASN'T MEANT
> FOR PRESIDENT
> OR MILLIONAIRE
>
> I'D BE CONTENT TO KNOW
> THAT EVERYWHERE I GO
> WHEN PEOPLE LOOK MY WAY
> THEY SIMPLY SAY
> "RESPECTABLE."

(Coming out of his reverie, **DICK** *finishes the shine with his usual flair.)*

CARLISLE. I was right. You do have talent.

DICK. Thank you, sir.

(He pays **DICK** *and exits.* **DICK** *palms the coin and begins to neatly pack up his rag and polish. When he finally looks at the coin,* **DICK**'s *eyes grow in wonder. Holding up the coin...)*

A dime! What a beautiful thing!

(His eye is caught by an elegant suit in a store window. **DICK** *paces in front of the window, staring at the suit covetously.)*

DICK. *(cont.)*
> AT FIRST YOU EARN A NICKEL
> WHICH SOON BECOMES A DIME
> A FLOOD STARTS WITH A TRICKLE
> IT ONLY TAKES TIME.

(During the following set change, we once again witness the activity of the busy street outside. **MICKEY** *is seen still pursuing his last* **CUSTOMER**, *"Hey, a shine is a nickel!"* **OFFICER FOY** *comes to the rescue of the frightened* **MAN** *as* **MICKEY** *disappears. Eventually, we are in the store.)*

Scene Two

(SETTING: The main salon of **SILAS SNOBDEN**'s *haberdashery. Bolts of cloth, suits, cravats, gloves and shirt are in evidence as are a cash register and a brand new type-writer. There's an entrance door, one to the stockroom and another to Snobden's office. A large stack of boxes is piled high in one corner.)*

(The window display has now rotated stage left or right. **DICK** *can still be seen on the outside examining the suit.)*

(TIME: Immediately following.)

(AT RISE: **CHAPIN** *is at the door, yelling after a departing male figure.* **HIGGINS** *is dozing in a corner.)*

CHAPIN. Thank you, sir. *(Customer leaves.)* Higgins!

HIGGINS. I wasn't asleep, Mr. Chapin. I was just resting my eyes.

CHAPIN. Never mind that! Finish Mr. Snobden's letter that you've been typewriting for two days.

HIGGINS. *(goes to typewriter, sits)* I caught my typewriting finger in the machine.

CHAPIN. Well, be more careful. Those machines are expensive.

*(***HIGGINS** *hunts and pecks through the following.* **DICK** *enters, recognizes* **CHAPIN** *from previous scene.)*

DICK. Oh, hello.

CHAPIN. You again! We have no need of a bootblack.

DICK. I ain't here as a bootblack. I was interested in that suit you have in the window.

CHAPIN. You're joking.

*(***SNOBDEN** *enters from his office.)*

SNOBDEN. Mr. Chapin!

CHAPIN. Good Morning, Mr. Snobden.

SNOBDEN. *(indicating the pile of boxes)* None of these orders has been delivered yet?

CHAPIN. I'll send Higgins as soon as he completes your letter. It's very difficult being without an office boy.

SNOBDEN. Still practicing, Higgins? That's good.

DICK. Excuse me, sir. About the suit – I could start with the handkerchief in the pocket. I can afford that.

CHAPIN. Really! I have no time for this nonsense.

SNOBDEN. Mr. Chapin!

CHAPIN. Very well. I'll get you a handkerchief.

DICK. I'd like the one in the window.

CHAPIN. It is not our policy to disturb the window.

SNOBDEN. Why isn't it? If that's the one the boy wants.

CHAPIN. Of course. Higgins! You can give your finger a rest.

HIGGINS. Yes, Mr. Chapin. (*He gets the colorful handkerchief from the window.*)

CHAPIN. That will be eight cents.

(**DICK** *hands* **CHAPIN** *a coin.* **CHAPIN** *quickly makes change at the register, gives* **DICK** *the change.*)

DICK. I'll be back to buy another piece as soon as I can. (*At the door,* **DICK** *stops to adjust the handkerchief in his pocket.*)

SNOBDEN. (*taking a package from the pile*) Higgins, deliver this package to Jacob Garrett and Company.

HIGGINS. I can't, Mr. Snobden.

SNOBDEN. "Can't!" There's no such word.

HIGGINS. I can't because they're closed.

CHAPIN. Garrett and Company will reopen on Wednesday. They're painting the premises.

DICK. Excuse me, sir – but they are open today.

CHAPIN. No, they are not.

DICK. Mr. Garrett's one of my regulars. I shined his shoes yesterday. He told me they're working around the painters.

SNOBDEN. Do you know his address?

DICK. 21 Maiden Lane.

SNOBDEN. *(bringing two other packages to* **DICK***)* Do you know where these are?

DICK. *(effortlessly)* This one'd be two blocks down Nassau past Beekman and Ann, right on Fulton, thirty-four's on the south side. Then down Nassau two more blocks, past Maiden Lane and John Street, left on Liberty, and number forty-five's on the north.

(**HIGGINS**, *impressed, almost applauds at this.*)

SNOBDEN. What's your name?

DICK. Richard Hunter.

SNOBDEN. Tell me, Hunter, have you ever worked in haberdashery?

DICK. No, sir. I've never been to New Jersey.

SNOBDEN. *(smiling)* No, no. A men's clothing establishment.

DICK. Oh, no. My line's been matches, newspapers, and shoes.

SNOBDEN. Estimable variety. Excellent. I need an office boy who must be honest, reliable, enterprising and does not gamble. My instincts tell me you have all these qualities.

CHAPIN. Mr. Snobden!

SNOBDEN. Well, Hunter? Will you accept the post?

DICK. I'm considerin', sir. But I do have a lot of clients on Wall Street who look to me for their appearance.

SNOBDEN. You will receive a new set of clothes and four dollars every Saturday.

DICK. Regular?

SNOBDEN. Rain or shine, every week.

DICK. I'll take it!

SNOBDEN. Good. Chapin, the position is filled. Higgins, fetch the coat. Hunter cannot represent this firm in that outfit.

(**HIGGINS** *exits to the stockroom.*)

DICK. I'll clean up real good, sir. You'll see.

SNOBDEN. We have some odd-sized suits in the stockroom that haven't sold. You can pick one out this evening when you've finished your work.

(**HIGGINS** *enters with the* **SILAS SNOBDEN** *jacket and lays it on the counter.*)

DICK. *(to* **CHAPIN***)* I've never had a salary before!

CHAPIN. Really? How sweet.

Song - SILAS SNOBDEN, INC.

WE ALL OF US HAVE JOBS TO DO
AND ALL OF THEM ARE LARGE,
BUT NO ONE'S MORE IMPORTANT THAN MYSELF,
THE CLERK-IN-CHARGE!

HIGGINS.

YOURS TRULY RUNS THE STOCK ROOM
AND I RUN IT LIKE A KING!
IT'S ORGANIZED SO NO ONE ELSE BUT ME
CAN FIND A THING!

BOTH.

WE REPRESENT THE SNOBDEN CLAN,
WE'LL SHARE THE SNOBDEN WAYS –
WHEN YOU BECOME A SNOBDEN MAN,
YOU'LL BASK IN SNOBDEN RAYS!

THE NAME OF SILAS SNOBDEN
IS THE VERY BEST IN TOWN
AND WHEN YOU JOIN OUR BROTHERHOOD
YOU MUST NOT LET US DOWN!

(hand over heart)

AND WE ARE TALL,
AND WE ARE PROUD
TO FACE THE WORLD WITHOUT A BLINK!
FOR WE'RE OVERJOYED
JUST TO BE EMPLOYED
BY SILAS SNOBDEN, INC.!

HIGGINS.

WHEN YOU ARRIVE AT 8 O'CLOCK
YOU'LL SWEEP THE FLOORS AND THEN,
WHEN YOU HAVE FINISHED SWEEPING THEM
YOU'LL SWEEP THEM ONCE AGAIN.

CHAPIN.
>AND WHEN THOSE FLOORS ARE NICE AND CLEAN
>YOU'LL BE ALLOWED TO STOP

BOTH.
>AND PUTTING DOWN YOUR TRUSTY BROOM
>YOU'LL THEN PICK UP YOUR MOP!
>
>YOU'LL POLISH BRASS!
>YOU'LL POLISH GLASS!
>AND IF YOU DO NOT SHIRK
>
>YOU'LL FINISH ALL YOU HAVE TO DO
>IN TIME TO START *YOUR* WORK!
>
>*(They hand off the broom and mop to* **DICK.***)*

CHAPIN.
>YOU'LL CLEAN OUT SHELVES!

HIGGINS.
>AND CLEAN OUT DRAWERS!

CHAPIN.
>AND MAYBE VERY SOON

BOTH.
>YOU'LL BE ALLOWED TO CLEAN OUT
>MISTER SNOBDEN'S OWN SPITTOON!

SNOBDEN. *(re-entering, more spoken and relaxed)*
>YOUR HOURS ARE FROM EIGHT TO SIX
>WITH TIME FOR LUNCH AT TWO –
>AND HOW YOU SPEND THOSE FIFTEEN MINUTES,
>SON, IS UP TO YOU!

DICK.
>GOD BLESS YOU, MISTER SNOBDEN!
>YOU'RE A HERO, ALL UNSUNG –

CHAPIN, HIGGINS, SNOBDEN.
>WE WISH WE HAD ADVANTAGES LIKE YOURS
>WHEN WE WERE YOUNG!

SNOBDEN. Chapin, the jacket!

DICK.
    AND I'LL BE TALL!
    AND I'LL BE PROUD!

OTHERS.
    YES, YOU'LL BE TALL!
    YES, YOU'LL BE PROUD!

ALL.
    AND LIFE IS GRAND

DICK.
    AS IT CAN BE!
    FOR THE OFFICE BOY
    WHO'S THE OFFICE BOY

OTHERS.
    FOR THE OFFICE BOY
    WHO'S THE OFFICE BOY

ALL.
    AT SILAS SNOBDEN,
    AT SILAS SNOBDEN,
    AT SNOBDEN
    I... N... C.!

(During the final measures, **DICK** *is loaded up with the pile of undelivered packages and shoved out the door. The door slam co-ordinates with the last note of music.)*

Scene Three

*(SETTING: The street in front of **SNOBDEN**'s store.)*

(TIME: Immediately following.)

*(AT RISE: **DICK** hurriedly leaves the shop and bangs smack into **LUKE GERRISH**, who is crossing. As **GERRISH** brushes himself off, he suddenly recognizes **DICK**.)*

GERRISH. Well, well. This is my lucky day.

DICK. Gerrish? Luke Gerrish?!

GERRISH. That's right, son.

DICK. So you're free? All paid up?

GERRISH. That's how it works. You do your time, you come home.

DICK. I'll have to move to Brooklyn. New York ain't safe no more.

GERRISH. Nah, I've been what they call "re-ha-bil-i-ta-ted." You're lookin' good.

DICK. I'm off the street. I got a job.

GERRISH. I see that. "SNOBDEN's." Nice coat they give you.

DICK. I'm just office boy. Don't go gettin' no fancy ideas.

GERRISH. Look at you. You're all grown up now.

DICK. You've been gone for three years. That's what happens.

GERRISH. C'mon, Dick. Give your old dad a smile.

DICK. My dad is dead.

GERRISH. I know that. I know I ain't him, but I'll have to do, son. Oh, I'm so sorry we lost her. It must have been rough on you. You were close to your ma. It was rough on me, too. My own wife, and I couldn't show up at her funeral. But of course I was – how they say – otherwise detained.

DICK. When you lived with us, you were always goin' off. Then you'd come home. The week after that, you'd be gone again. And you know what? She was better off without you.

GERRISH. She didn't think so. She wrote and told me that. Many times.

DICK. Well, she's not around so we'll never know, will we?

GERRISH. Give me a chance to make things up to you. For your ma's sake.

DICK. You ain't Irish, Luke, but you sure got the gift.

GERRISH. I know life ain't been easy. Now I'm back, I can show you the ropes. Since I'm out, I've found me a lady I like. Why don't you come with me now? You can meet her.

DICK. I can't.

GERRISH. I have big plans for us. I been lookin' for you.

DICK. Don't make plans, Luke. I got my own plans. Your ways didn't quite work out, did they? I kinda like it here – on the outside. Good luck, Luke.

(He gathers up the packages.)

GERRISH. You always was a dreamer, kid. When you gonna wise up?

Song - *COCK AND BULL*

(casually)

IF A MAN IS BOTH LAZY AND POOR,
THEN THERE ISN'T A BIT OF A DOUBT
WHAT THEY'RE CALLING HIM, YOU CAN BE SURE,
IS A SHIFTLESS AND INDOLENT LOUT –

BUT IF LUCKILY HE WAS BORN RICH,
NO ONE BOTHERS TO NAG OR TO PROD
"SHOE A HORSE! CARRY BRICKS! DIG A DITCH!"
HE'S HIS LORDSHIP OF LEISURE, BY GOD!

SO THE DIFFERENCE IS SIMPLE AND SWEET,
AND AN IDLER YOU ARE OR ARE NOT
IF YOU IDLE ALL DAY ON A STREET,
OR YOU IDLE ALL DAY ON A YACHT!

OH, THE COCK AND BULL GOES ON AND ON
AND THEY TAKE US ALL FOR FOOLS!
AND WHAT YOU'RE CALLED FOR WHAT YOU DO
DEPENDS ON WHO'S MAKING THE RULES, THE RULES –
DEPENDS ON WHO'S MAKING THE RULES!

*(Two of **GERRISH**'s **OLD CRONIES** enter.)*

FIRST CRONY (MAN #4). Well, look who they sent back to society.

*(One of the **CRONIES** circles **DICK**, examining the boxes. **DICK** grabs the packages away from him.)*

SECOND CRONY (MAN #1). Gerrish! What'd they get you for? Petty larceny, wasn't it?

GERRISH. Not even close. Armed robbery. Then they threw the book at me.

FIRST CRONY. It's a cruel world. Look at you. Three years for armed robbery.

SECOND CRONY. Yeah. You're doin' somethin' wrong.

GERRISH. You're right about that. I didn't reach high enough.

(with more anger now)

IF THEY'RE MISSING A DOLLAR OR TWO,
OH, I KNOW WHO'LL GET ALL OF THE BLAME –
IF I'M CAUGHT, I KNOW JUST WHAT THEY'LL DO
'CAUSE I'M ON TO THE RULES OF THE GAME –

BUT IF I CAN BE CRAFTY WITH GUILE
AS I JUGGLE THE BOOKS OF A BANK,
OR I SKIN YOU ALIVE WHILE YOU SMILE,
I'M A CROOK OF A MUCH HIGHER RANK!

SO IT'S ALL IN THE WAY THAT YOU ROB
THAT WILL MAKE YOU RISE UP OR GO DOWN –
STEAL A HUNDRED, YOU BUNGLE THE JOB –
STEAL A MILLION, YOU'RE RUNNING THE TOWN!

WHILE THE COCK AND BULL GOES ON AND ON
AND THERE'S NEVER ANY PAUSE –
AND WHAT YOU'RE CALLED FOR WHAT YOU DO
DEPENDS ON WHO'S WRITING THE LAWS, THE LAWS –
DEPENDS ON WHO'S WRITING THE LAWS!

*(The **CRONIES** flee, as does **DICK** in the other direction.)*

GERRISH. *(cont.)*
>TELL ME, WILL I LIVE A LIFE OF EASE
>OR A LIFE BEHIND A LOCK?
>THAT, MY FRIEND, WILL ALWAYS DEPEND
>ON WHO IS DEFINING THE COCK AND BULL –
>WHO IS DEFINING, WHO IS DEFINING –
>DEFINING THE COCK AND BULL!

(blackout)

Scene Four

*(SETTING: A street near **MRS. McHUGH**'s boarding house.)*

(TIME: Late afternoon of the same day.)

*(AT RISE: A **VENDOR** of knick knacks and gewgaws sees **STACIA**, who is carrying a bag of groceries. Another lady **CUSTOMER** is by the vendor's stall.)*

VENDOR (WOMAN #1). Stacia! I found one! Where've you been? Come see!

STACIA. Molly, the lantern?!

VENDOR. I found it on Mott Street. Just like you described it too, with a candle.

(She holds up an ornate paper Chinese lantern.)

STACIA. Oh, it's beautiful. It reminds me of some far away mysterious place.

VENDOR. Honey, it was made in Buffalo.

STACIA. Is it expensive?

VENDOR. It's got a little nick on it, which you can hardly see. Two bits too much?

STACIA. No! And thanks for remembering.

CUSTOMER (WOMAN #3). Don't you have someone to buy things for you?

STACIA. Oh, I have someone. He's just not the lantern-buying sort.

VENDOR. A girl like you deserves better.

*(**STACIA** moves away from the stall. She sits and examines the lantern as she sings to the **CUSTOMER**, who has sat down next to her. The **VENDOR** comes over, too.)*

Song - *MAYBE TODAY*

STACIA.
ONE OF THESE DAYS
HE'LL TELL ME HE LOVES ME –
MAYBE TODAY –

*(The **VENDOR** has heard this before. The **CUSTOMER** is more sympathetic. **STACIA** continues.)*

STACIA. *(cont.)*
ONE OF THESE DAYS
HE'S CERTAIN TO SAY IT –
MAYBE TOMORROW –

WHY IS IT SO IMPORTANT TO HEAR
THOSE WORDS STILL UNSAID
WHEN EVERY DAY I HEAR THEM SO CLEARLY
INSIDE MY HEAD?

DREAMS CAN COME TRUE
AND WISHES GET GRANTED –
MAYBE TODAY –

MIRACLES TOO
ARE WAITING TO HAPPEN –
MAYBE TOMORROW –

MAYBE TOMORROW
TURNS INTO NEVER!
I COULD WAIT A LIFETIME,
I COULD WAIT FOREVER,

BUT MAYBE HE'LL SAY
HE LOVES ME TODAY.

*(**STACIA** gets up to leave. The **CUSTOMER** by her side speaks.)*

CUSTOMER. Good luck to you, Stacia.

*(**STACIA** crosses, and runs into **MRS. McHUGH**, her landlady, who is just leaving the boarding house.)*

McHUGH (WOMAN #2). Stacia! Oh you gave me a start! Where were you?! You were out all afternoon.

STACIA. It's Thursday. I sew for Mrs. Hartley on Thursday.

McHUGH. Well, your "cousin" or whatever he is, didn't like it. He asked me three times if I'd seen you.

STACIA. Maybe he's got news of work. He's got prospects. Any day now.

McHUGH. I rented the room to you, not him. And he was askin' for you in a most un-cousinly way. You must be very close.

STACIA. He's got nowhere else to go. Mrs. McHugh, you know that.

(She hums to herself as **McHUGH** *continues.)*

McHUGH. I don't know anything! And what I don't know can't hurt me, now can it? If you're wise, you'll get a little less close. Hopin' is one thing, Stacia, dreamin' is another.

*(***McHUGH*** exits.)*

STACIA.
WHY IS IT SO IMPORTANT TO HEAR
THOSE WORDS STILL UNSAID
WHEN EVERY DAY I HEAR THEM SO CLEARLY
INSIDE MY HEAD?

(In the distance, for a few moments, we can see **GERRISH** *in an angry and violent confrontation with a stranger.)*

DREAMS CAN COME TRUE
AND WISHES GET GRANTED –
MAYBE TODAY –

MIRACLES TOO
ARE WAITING TO HAPPEN –
MAYBE TOMORROW!

MAYBE TOMORROW
TURNS INTO NEVER –
I COULD WAIT A LIFETIME –
I COULD WAIT FOREVER –

BUT MAYBE HE'LL SAY HE
LOVES ME TODAY.

(She exits into the house.)

Scene Five

*(**SETTING**: In front of the Wall Street Saloon.)*

*(**TIME**: Around 6:30 pm that evening.)*

*(**AT RISE**: The street life resumes. A group of **WOMEN** crosses, **GERRISH** hurriedly passes them going the other way. He flirts with one and continues on his way. **FOSWELL** is peddling shines. **DICK** enters, now dressed in a very ill-fitting but new coat and trousers from **SNOBDEN**'s.)*

FOSWELL. *(to **DICK**)* Shine'em up, sir? Only two cents.

DICK. Foswell?! Next thing you'll be payin' *them.*

FOSWELL. This morning you were in rags!

DICK. I have a position now. I'm in habadeeshery.

FOSWELL. Haba-what-ery?

DICK. I deliver things. And when I do, I get a tip. Today? Two bits. And when I have dough, I spread it around. Dinner on me.

FOSWELL. Thanks a lot. Where will we go?

DICK. Well –

*(**TWO YOUNG BUCKS** enter the saloon. **DICK** overhears them.)*

FIRST BUCK (MAN #1). Do you think I should convert my Preferred to the Common on the Erie Railroad?

SECOND BUCK (MAN #4). They say the Common is heading north. Of course, you never know.

FIRST BUCK. Thanks. That helps a lot.

DICK. If you keep your ears open, the answer comes. We're eating here!

(And we are now inside The Wall Street Saloon.)

Scene Six

*(**SETTING**: The Wall Street Saloon.)*

*(**TIME**: Immediately following.)*

*(**AT RISE**: A bar and coffee house catering to the young men of the business world. Signs on the wall: "Oyster Pie – 15¢," "Beefsteak – 20¢," "Coffee – 3¢." **FOSWELL** and **DICK** enter, taking it all in.)*

FOSWELL. We don't belong here.

DICK. You belong wherever you are. Let's sit down.

FOSWELL. *(looks around)* They're staring at us.

DICK. That's because we're unusual – we're interestin'.

WAITER (MICKEY). *(approaching)* Wouldn't you lads be more comfortable at our lunch counter?

FOSWELL. I told you –

DICK. No, we would not! So without further fuss, two oyster pies and two coffees.

WAITER (MICKEY). Suit yourself.

(He crosses to counter.)

DICK. He's kinda high and mighty, ain't he?

FOSWELL. Well, a little presumptuous.

DICK. *(taking out a pencil and card)* Write that down.

FOSWELL. Write what down?

DICK. "Pre-sumpt…whatever." Wonderful word. I must find a home for it.

FOSWELL. It's no good to you until you can use it in a sentence.

*(He hands card back as the **WAITER** approaches.)*

WAITER (MICKEY). Two oyster pies, two coffees.

DICK. Thank you. Your service was excellent. Even presumptuous.

*(The **WAITER** reacts and exits.)*

Wrong?

FOSWELL. Wrong.

DICK. *(as he eats)* See what I mean? That sorta thing is holdin' me back. You see those gents all around? They know things I need to know.

FOSWELL. They're not going to talk to us.

DICK. Watch!

*(He looks around, sees **FIRST BUCK** eyeing him)*

Excuse me, sir. As I came in I could not help overhearing. Were you considering converting to the Erie Railroad Common?

FIRST BUCK (MAN #1). Uh – yes, I was.

DICK. Good! You should. The Common's goin' through the roof. I heard that on the street.

FIRST BUCK. Thank you!

FOSWELL. What did that mean?

DICK. I have no idea.

*(**FIRST BUCK** crosses to **DICK**.)*

FIRST BUCK. Excuse me, sir. I'm with Milbanks and Murphy.

DICK. Are you now? I'm with Foswell.

FIRST BUCK. I'm sorry. I don't know him.

DICK. Of Hunter and Foswell.

FIRST BUCK. Oh, yes! An excellent firm.

DICK. Thank you. I'm Hunter. President. Foswell is our D.I.P.

FIRST BUCK. Didn't get that.

DICK. Director of Investment Planning.

FIRST BUCK. Oh! How do you do. Would you like one of our prospectuses?

DICK. Well, I don't know. What do you think, Foswell?

FOSWELL. We're not here on business, Hunter. I don't think so.

FIRST BUCK. Of course. Forgive me. Here's my card. If I can ever be of service –

DICK. Thank you. We'll keep you in mind.

(**FIRST BUCK** *returns to his table, then, to* **FOSWELL**...)

Good. Now we've won their attention.

FOSWELL. Yes. How do we lose it?

DICK. We don't. *(directed to the room)* Big future, the Erie. We made a wise move when we converted to the Common. So one day I'll sell some of my shares and maybe open a place like this one.

FIRST BUCK. This kid's loaded!

SECOND BUCK (MAN #4). And he's talking acquisitions!

THIRD BUCK (MAN #3). *(fumbling in his pocket)* I've got a prospectus for him.

Song - *PUT YOUR MONEY IN*

FOURTH BUCK (MAN #2). *(offering a prospectus)*
>PUT YOUR MONEY IN STOCK
>AND YOU CAN UNLOCK
>THE DOOR TO RICHES
>INDULGING EACH WHIM –

THIRD BUCK. *(with another prospectus)*
>BUY A CORPORATE BOND
>UNLESS YOU ARE FOND
>OF DIGGING DITCHES!
>DON'T LISTEN TO HIM –

FIRST BUCK. *(still another)*
>I CAN'T BELIEVE WHAT I'VE HEARD
>NOW HERE'S SOME LOVELY PREFERRED
>IT'S PAID A DIVIDEND THROUGH THICK AND THROUGH THIN –
>
>AND IF THE MARKET GOES "CRASH"
>YOU'LL STILL HAVE PLENTY OF CASH
>SO YOU CAN
>LIVE LIKE A LORD,
>NICELY AFFORD
>ANY EXPENSIVE SIN!

SECOND BUCK.
>BUT I SAY
>PUT YOUR MONEY IN WINE
>THE VALUE IS FINE
>AND EVERY BUBBLE
>WILL ADD TO YOUR STAKE –

FIRST BUCK.
>CALIFORNIA'S GRAND!
>EACH DOLLAR IN LAND
>OUT THERE WILL DOUBLE

OTHERS.
>UNTIL IT GOES QUAKE!

ALL FOUR.
>IF YOU WILL
>MAKE A LITTLE INVESTMENT
>TAKE A FLYER OR TWO –
>YOU'LL DISCOVER
>YOU'LL FEEL BRAND NEW!
>
>JUST DON'T GO
>FEELIN' FUNNY IN
>PUTTIN' MONEY IN –
>NEVER CATCH A BEAR UNLESS YOU
>PUT A LITTLE HONEY IN
>ALL FOR YOU!

DICK. *(considering, to* **FOSWELL***)* Yes?

FOSWELL. No!

FIRST BUCK.
>PUT YOUR MONEY IN OIL
>YOU'LL EASILY FOIL
>A BAD DEPRESSION –
>I'M TELLIN' YOU, BUD!

OTHER THREE.
>KEEP AWAY FROM HIS OIL!
>THEY NEVER HIT OIL
>ON HIS CONCESSION –
>THEY ONLY HIT MUD!

FOURTH BUCK.

> I KNOW A PROSPECTIN' MAN
> WHO WENT OUT WEST WITH A PAN
> AND NOW THAT MINER IS AS RICH AS CAN BE!
> I'LL SELL YOU ALL OF HIS SHARES –
> THEY'LL ANSWER ALL OF YOUR PRAYERS,

SECOND BUCK.

> OR YOU CAN
> TEAR 'EM UP SMALL,
> HANG ON THE WALL
> OUT IN THE OLD PRIV-EE!

FIRST BUCK.

> HEY, LISTEN –
> I KNOW SEVERAL MEN
> WHO HAVE AN INVENTION TO UNRAVEL
> ALL HISTORY'S COURSE!

SECOND BUCK.

> DON'T YOU COVER THAT BET!
> THEY THINK THEY CAN GET
> A CART TO TRAVEL
> WITHOUT ANY HORSE!

ALL BUCKS.

> IF YOU WILL
> TRY A LITTLE ADVENTURE,
> TAKE A GAMBLE OR TWO –
> YOU'LL DISCOVER
> YOU'LL FEEL BRAND NEW!
>
> JUST DON'T GO
> FEELIN' FUNNY IN
> PUTTIN' MONEY IN –
> MONEY'S LIKE A KINDA DAY YOU'RE
> FEELIN' NICE'N SUNNY IN
> ALL FOR YOU!
>
> WE'VE A SECRET TO TELL:
> SOME PEOPLE WOULD SELL
> MOST ANY OLD STOCK
> TO ANY YOUNG PUP!

ALL BUCKS. *(cont.)*
>BUT WE'RE HAPPY TO SAY
>WE AREN'T THAT WAY
>WE'VE ALWAYS SOLD STOCK
>THAT ONLY GOES UP!
>
>IF YOU WILL
>TRY A LITTLE ADVENTURE,
>TAKE A FLYER OR TWO,
>YOU'LL DISCOVER
>YOU'LL FEEL BRAND NEW

DICK & FOSWELL. *(can't resist)*
>JUST DON'T GO
>FEELIN' FUNNY IN
>PUTTIN' MONEY IN –

ALL.
>SOON IT'S GONNA MULTIPLY
>LIKE BUNNIES WHO KEEP BUNNYIN'
>ALL FOR YOU!

*(Enjoying the moment, **DICK** accepts all of their prospectuses. By the end of the number he has accumulated quite a stack of them. He and **FOSWELL** leave the saloon as **MRS. MOONEY**'s stoop appears.)*

Scene Seven

*(**SETTING**: Moving into the stoop and street outside **MRS. MOONEY**'s boarding house on Mott Street. A "Room To Let" sign is in the first floor window.)*

*(**TIME**: Immediately following.)*

*(**AT RISE**: **DICK** and **FOSWELL** run on.)*

DICK. Wasn't that a treat?

FOSWELL. I am your D.I.P.???

DICK. You couldn't be President. I'm President.

FOSWELL. If I'm D.I.P. how come I'm down to two cents a shine? You make a lot more.

DICK. I ain't troubled with bashfulness.

FOSWELL. So what do I do?

DICK. Well, first we gotta find you a personality. You're kinda scrawny. We can use that. And all I know about readin' and writin' you could put in a nutshell. So if you'll teach me reading in the evenin's, I'll wise you up on the bootblack business. What do you say?

FOSWELL. Foswell and Hunter?

DICK. Hunter and Foswell!

*(They shake. **FOSWELL** exits. **DICK** overhears **MRS. MOONEY** and remains. **MRS. MOONEY** emerges, holding a **YOUNG MAN** (**MAN #2**) by the ear as she escorts him out of the house.)*

MOONEY. No more excuses! I told you three times I do not allow whiskey on the premises. So get out! And don't come back!

*(The **YOUNG MAN** runs off.)*

But may the Lord keep you in his hand and never close his fist too tight!

DICK. Top of the evenin', Madam. Is the lady of the house at home?

MOONEY. Who wants to know?

DICK. I might be interested in leasin' that room.

MOONEY. Oh, Sweet Jesus, another rotten apple.

DICK. What's the matter with me?

MOONEY. I was hopin' to find me an older gentleman –

DICK. I'm growin' older by the minute.

MOONEY. – who's a teetotaler.

DICK. Never touch the stuff. The name's Richard Hunter, E.S.Q.

MOONEY. Finola May Mooney, M.R.S. Mr. Mooney's out west – prospectin' for gold or somethin' – but he could be back – any minute.

DICK. Is there a room?

MOONEY. I don't think it will do you. It's a very small room.

DICK. I don't move much when I sleep. And I'd be out most of the time – at business.

MOONEY. What is your business, if I might inquire?

DICK. Oh, I'm a professional.

MOONEY. Indeed! Professional what?

DICK. Gentleman's furnishings.

MOONEY. And did you get those at your business?

DICK. *(adjusting the much too-long sleeves)* I'm just givin' an airin' to some odd sizes that don't get out much.

(**DICK** *opens his jacket to adjust it and show the fancy inner lining. He takes the thick pack of prospectuses from the pocket.*)

MOONEY. What are those?

DICK. Just some Wall Street prospectuses. Always keep 'em here, next to my heart.

MOONEY. Oh. Well!

Song - *THE ROOM*

THE ROOM ISN'T LARGE
AND IT'S NOT OVER-SUNNY –
THE FLOOR KIND OF WAVES
AND THE CEILING SLANTS FUNNY –
BUT, BUCKO, ME BOY
IT'S THE BEST FOR THE MONEY
YOU'LL PAY –

MOONEY. *(cont.)*
> IT ISN'T A CASTLE
> IN CORK OR KILKENNY –
> BUT BETTER THAN MOONEY'S
> YOU'RE NOT FINDIN' ANY
> FOR GETTIN' YOUR MONEY'S WORTH
> DOWN TO THE PENNY
> I SAY –
>
> YOU CAN EAT HERE AS WELL, IF YOU CARE TO –
> IF YOU'RE PARTIAL TO IRISH LAMB STEW –
> WITH PLENTY OF CABBAGE AND LOTS OF POTATOES –
> THERE'S EVEN SOME LAMB IN IT, TOO!
>
> YOU'LL GET A FRESH TOWEL
> ON THE DOT, EVERY SUNDAY –
> TWO SPANKIN' CLEAN SHEETS
> EVERY FOURTH OR FIFTH MONDAY –
> THE WEEK STARTS ON SUNDAY
> AND SUNDAY'S JUST ONE DAY
> AWAY –
>
> SO, DEAR MISTER HUNTER,
> YOU'D BETTER MOVE IN BY
> TODAY!

DICK. Sounds perfect, Mrs. Mooney. How much?

MOONEY. You mean you don't want to see it first? Actually, that's wise.
> A SMART GENT LIKE YOU
> CAN'T BE LIED TO OR LED ON –
> I MEET ALL ME OTHER
> COMPETITORS HEAD ON –
> AND IF I AM LYING,
> MAY GOD STRIKE ME DEAD ON
> THE SPOT!

(looking upwards, makes the sign of the cross, steps to her side)

> THE ROOM COMES COMPLETE
> WITH A WINDOW AND CURTAIN –
> I CLEAN IT MESELF

MOONEY. *(cont.)*
>WHEN ME BACK ISN'T HURTIN' –
>UNFORTUNATELY,
>ME POOR BACK HAS BEEN HURTIN'
>A LOT!

DICK. It has a real ceiling?

MOONEY. Well, most of me rooms do.
>THERE'S A VERY NICE CHEST WITH A MIRROR,
>SOME HOOKS, AND A HANDY WIDE SHELF –
>A COMFORTABLE BED,
>BUT NO SMOKING IN BED!
>IN FACT, NOTHIN' IN BED BUT YOURSELF! –
>
>THIS HOUSE, BEIN' IRISH,
>WHEN EVENIN' APPROACHES,
>YOU MIGHT SEE SOME ELVES
>RIDIN' WEE GOLDEN COACHES –
>AND LEPRECHAUNS DRESSED UP AS ROACHES,
>THOUGH ROACHES THEY'RE NOT!
>
>SO, DEAR MISTER HUNTER
>I COULD NOT BE BLUNTER –
>ME DEAR MISTER HUNTER,
>YOU BETTER MOVE IN LIKE A SHOT!

DICK. What's the rent?

MOONEY. I ought to have a dollar a week.

DICK. Say seventy-five cents and I'll take it.

MOONEY. A dollar, and I change the sheets every week.

DICK. Seventy-five, and you can change 'em twice a month.

MOONEY. You'll pay every week – in advance?

DICK. I will! *(He takes out some coins.)*

MOONEY. Ninety cents, and I'll make your bed.

DICK. Seventy-five, and I'll make it myself.

MOONEY. You know how?

DICK. I'll learn!

MOONEY. Done!

DICK. *(counting out coins)* Fifty…Seventy-five…

MOONEY. And the bath's down the hall, with hot water every single evening…from seven to seven-fifteen. *(She starts to exit again, turns back.)* Oh, silly me. I forgot. Here's your key. *(She gives him the key.)*

Song - *RESPECTABILITY*

DICK.
>A KEY TO CALL MY OWN,
>A DOOR THAT LOCKS –
>I MIGHT SLEEP EVEN BETTER IN A BED
>THAN IN A BOX –
>
>THE LAP O'LUXURY
>AND ALL COMPLETE –
>A BATHROOM, BEST OF ALL,
>THAT'S DOWN THE HALL
>NOT DOWN THE STREET –
>
>THIS LIFE IS NEW TO ME
>BUT I ALREADY SEE
>THIS ROOM AND I REFLECT
>COMPLETE RESPECTABILITY.

(Lights fade except on one of the upstairs windows. **DICK** *looks up and enters the house.)*

Scene Eight

(SETTING: MOONEY's stoop has disappeared and we are back on Wall Street. Entrance to the bank is prominent.)

(TIME: Several weeks later. Lunchtime.)

(AT RISE: A CROWD is gathering center stage, all staring in wonder across the street [into the audience] at something, murmuring underneath the music. Eventually, SILAS SNOBDEN enters and joins the crowd.)

WOMAN #1. Astonishing!

WOMAN #2. Incredible!

MAN #1. Have you been inside yet?

MAN #2. I'm taking the family tomorrow.

WOMAN #1. We've been in. Just this morning. You won't believe your eyes.

MAN #2. What will they think of next?

SNOBDEN. They'll think of something. The only thing constant is change.

(DICK and FOSWELL enter in the midst of their daily English lesson.)

DICK. *(reading from a prospectus)* "AD-MIN-IS-TRA-TORS" – "EX-EC-U-TORS" – "SUCCESSORS AND ASSIGNS..." What's this? AL-MO-GOSH-EN??

FOSWELL. Not "AL-MO-GOSH-EN," that's "AMALGAMATION."

(They have reached the CROWD and of course can't resist joining in the group stare. DICK notices SNOBDEN.)

DICK. Afternoon, Mr. Snobden. What's everyone staring at?

SNOBDEN. Most alarming! Most disturbing.

DICK. *(carefully reading the unseen sign)* F.- W. – WOOL – WORTH... What is it? What does it do?

SNOBDEN. Gives me heartburn.

FOSWELL. I read about it in the Herald. It's called a Five and Ten Cent Store!

DICK. (*pulls out his treasured handkerchief*) Other than my handkerchief, I don't think we have much of anything in our store that costs less than a dime. Do we Mr. Snobden? (**SILAS** *is in a daze.*) Mr. Snobden?

Song - *KEEPING UP WITH THE TIMES*

SNOBDEN.

> THIS PUTS US IN A DANGEROUS POSITION –
> THAT STORE ACROSS THE STREET COULD DO US IN –
> BUT SNOBDEN HAS NO SHORTAGE OF AMBITION –
> WE'LL CHALLENGE MISTER WOOLWORTH, AND WE'LL WIN!
>
> (*growing confident*)
>
> THERE ISN'T ANY REASON TO BE NERVOUS –
> IT'S SOMETIMES AN ADVANTAGE TO BE SMALL –
> WE'LL CONCENTRATE ON QUALITY AND SERVICE
> WHILE DOING THE MOST VITAL THING OF ALL:
>
> KEEPING UP THE TIMES,
> THAT'S THE BUSINESSMAN'S AIM –
> STAYING ONE STEP AHEAD
> OF THE CROWD OR YOU'RE DEAD
> AT THE MERCANTILE GAME –
>
> QUICKLY SPOTTING A TREND,
> THAT'S THE SMART THING TO DO –
> NEVER LOOKING BEHIND
> OR YOU'RE LIABLE TO FIND
> SOMEONE GAINING ON YOU –
>
> I'LL MAKE MY LIFELONG SACRED MISSION
> WITH A HAND THAT SURE AND DEFT,
> TO DEFEAT ALL COMPETITION
> TIL JUST SNOBDEN'S IS LEFT!
>
> LETTING RIVALS WIN OUT
> IS THE WORST OF ALL CRIMES –
> SO TO SETTLE THEIR HASH
> THEN RETIRE WITH YOUR CASH
> DOWN TO TROPICAL CLIMES
> YOU MUST KEEP UP WITH THE TIMES!

SNOBDEN. Back to work Hunter. Your lunch hour is only fifteen minutes.

DICK. I was on my way to open a bank account.

SNOBDEN. Oh. In that case, take an extra fifteen minutes. Nothing more important than a bank account.

FOSWELL. Yes there is. An education.

SNOBDEN. And a strong investment strategy, of course.

FOSWELL. First an education.

SNOBDEN. Yes, you – *(annoyed to* **FOSWELL***)* Who ARE you, young man!!

DICK. He's my personal tutor. He's been guiding me through world history, arithmetic, English grammar and the tax on sin.

FOSWELL. Syntax!

DICK. Exactly!

*(***HIGGINS** *enters, talking excitedly to another man, then to the* **CROWD***.)*

HIGGINS. It's a dilly of a store. There is stuff piled high on every counter. I've never seen such a place.

(sings with careful precision)

THEY'VE GOT
DRINKING CUPS AND STRAINERS –
BOXES, PURSES, AND CONTAINERS –
LATHER BRUSHES FULL OF BRISTLES –
LINEN THREAD, POLICEMENS' WHISTLES –
WOODEN LADDERS, FEATHER DUSTERS –
PAPER FLOWERS ALL IN CLUSTERS –
PANS FOR FRYING, PANS FOR BAKING –
TINS FOR SALT AND PEPPER SHAKING –

CUSTOMER #1 (WOMAN #1).

PLATES OF CHINA, GLASS OR METAL –

CUSTOMER #2 (MAN #2).

HERE'S A POT AND THERE'S A KETTLE –

CUSTOMER #3 (WOMAN #3).

PRETTY RED AND YELLOW JEWL'RY –

CUSTOMER #4 (MAN #4).
> OTHER FEMININE TOMFOOL'RY –

CUSTOMER #5 (WOMAN #4).
> HANDY IRON COVER LIFTERS –
> LEMON GRATERS, FLOUR SIFTERS –

CUSTOMER #6 (MAN #3).
> UNDER GARMENTS, TOP AND BOTTOM –

HIGGINS.
> IF YOU WANT 'EM, THEY HAVE GOT 'EM!

HIGGINS. (**HIGGINS** *has now come face to face with* **SNOBDEN**.)
> Mr. Snobden!

SNOBDEN. Higgins –

HIGGINS. You're looking very well, sir. I think you've lost some weight.

(No response, so he flees.)

DICK. *(learning)*
> KEEP AHEAD OF THE MOB
> AND YOU'LL CARRY THE DAY –

FOSWELL.
> YOU WILL NEVER KNOW WANT
> IF YOU STAY AU COURANT –

DICK.
> AS THE GERMANS WOULD SAY!

SNOBDEN & DICK & FOSWELL.
> LETTING RIVALS WIN OUT
> IS THE WORST OF ALL CRIMES!

ALL.
> SO TO SETTLE THEIR HASH
> AND RETIRE WITH YOUR CASH
> DOWN TO TROPICAL CLIMES,
> YOU MUST KEEP UP WITH THE TIMES!

*(**ALLEN CARSLISLE** has entered. He notices **SNOBDEN**.)*

CARLISLE. Silas, old man. How are you? Have you been inside the new Woolworths? Men's shirts, trousers, *(stops)* – But I wouldn't worry if I were you. There's still no finer haberdashery than yours.

SNOBDEN. And no friendlier bank than yours, Allen old man.

DICK. Holy mackerel, it's you!

CARLISLE. *(sees* **DICK***)* There you are! I've been looking for you! I went back the next day but you weren't there. I haven't had a good shine since.

SNOBDEN. You know each other?

CARLISLE. I tried a word out on you.

DICK	**CARLISLE**
Finesse!	Finesse!

DICK. I'm still lookin' for a home for it.

SNOBDEN. Hunter works for me now.

CARLISLE. You boys on your way to explore the new five and dime?

FOSWELL. No, sir. We're opening him a bank account.

SNOBDEN. His first.

DICK. I ain't no piker. I'm putting in three dollars.

CARLISLE. Well I appreciate your business.

>TO KEEP UP WITH THE TIMES
>SAVE WHATVER YOU CAN –
>BUILDING EACH LITTLE SUM
>IS THE WAY TO GO FROM
>RAGS TO RICHES, YOUNG MAN!

CROWD.

>AS YOUR DOLLARS ALL GROW
>OUT OF NICKELS AND DIMES
>YOU WILL KNOW WHAT TO THANK
>FOR THESE TRIPS TO THE BANK
>AS YOUR AFFLUENCE CLIMBS
>JUST KEEPING UP WITH THE TIMES!

DICK.

>WHEN BRAVE COLUMBUS WENT A-SAILING
>'CROSS THAT BIG AND SCARY SEA
>WITH HIS COURAGE NEVER FAILING
>HE HAD NOTHIN' ON ME!

(The doors to the bank open ceremoniously, **CARLISLE** *escorts* **DICK** *inside.)*

ALL.
SO LET'S HAPPILY RING
THOSE CENTENNIAL CHIMES –
IF WE STAY IN THE LEAD
WE ARE BOUND TO SUCCEED
FOR AMERICA RHYMES
WITH KEEPING UP WITH THE TIMES!
WITH KEEPING UP WITH THE TIMES!

*(***DICK*** emerges, holding up as a grand prize, his new bankbook. Everyone returns to work. The street clears. Time passes.)*

Scene Nine

*(**SETTING**: **STACIA**'s room in **MRS. McHUGH**'s boarding house.)*

*(**TIME**: An evening in late June.)*

*(**AT RISE**: **GERRISH** pours a drink, stares out the window where the lantern is now hung. **STACIA** enters, carrying a few paper flowers.)*

GERRISH. Where you been?

STACIA. I've been working. A wedding. In Yonkers. You know that.

GERRISH. That was yesterday.

STACIA. I wasn't finished. They asked me to stay. Were you worried? Glory be, did you miss me?

(She puts the flowers in an old vase.)

GERRISH. I was surprised is all. No, it gave me a night off. To hit the hot spots, which you don't like.

STACIA. I see.

(She knows it's a lie; better not go there.)

It was a grand wedding. She was a June bride and she looked – Oh, Luke, she came down a staircase in the dress I made and I thought "some day I'll make one just like it – for me!"

GERRISH. Everything is romance with you. What's wrong with what is?

STACIA. Nothing. I don't mind the sewing to pay the rent and keep us in food, but what's wrong with what could be?

GERRISH. I got a few "could be's" of my own.

STACIA. Yes, you've told me, every day. But you never talk about your past. I'm the dreamer? All I hear from you are plans – for us.

GERRISH. It is "us." I went out today and I found myself by the river, by the place where you and I first saw each other. I was with some pals, you were with a lady friend. That was just two months ago tomorrow.

STACIA. You remember the date?

GERRISH. See? I got some romance in me too. That day, you dropped something.

STACIA. A small box with some thread in it.

GERRISH. And when I picked it up and handed it to you, our eyes met. And suddenly we were all alone. No more pals, no more lady friend. We knew.

Song - MAYBE TODAY (reprise)

STACIA. *(unsure)*
DREAMS CAN COME TRUE
AND WISHES GET GRANTED –
MAYBE TODAY –

GERRISH. It's like that first day with us. When anything was possible. And we're still there. It's been good.

STACIA. *(giving in)*
MIRACLES TOO
ARE WAITING TO HAPPEN –
MAYBE TOMORROW –

(Music continues under.)

GERRISH. I'll take care of everything. We'll be fine. What do you say?

(She looks at him.)

Are you with me?

(They kiss. The lights fade till only the glow of the lantern is left.)

Scene Ten

(SETTING: Limbo. A street in Lower Manhattan.)

(TIME: Late May.)

(AT RISE: FOSWELL is sitting alone by his shoeshine box. It has a sign on it: "Final Sale During June Only – Shine 1¢". MICKEY MAGUIRE enters, newspapers under his arm.)

MICKEY. "Extra! Grant Visits New Jersey." Read all about it!

FOSWELL. Where's your shoeshine box?

MICKEY. I couldn't pay the rent with cigar butts, so now I'm in the news trade. But business ain't so good. President Grant in New Jersey don't stir the blood. Looks like you ain't doin' no better.

FOSWELL. What am I, invisible? Dick said I should make people notice me, but I don't know how.

MICKEY. "Dick said." Ha! He got lucky. He's off the slag pile, ain't he though? Gentlemen's furnishin's, imagine that. But he always knew how to get noticed, I gotta give him that. When he was a newsboy, before he took on shoes, he used to say, "If the news ain't interestin', make interestin' news!" His last headline was: "Queen Victoria Assassinated!" Sold out quick on that one. Hey, wait a minute, that's it…

(Music begins.)

(He calls out.)

Extra! Get it here first! "President Grant Declares War…"

(CROWD shrugs.)

…on Canada!"

(CROWD explodes with excitement, descends on MICKEY.)

…Read all about it! "Border Closed, USA-Canadian War!"

*(Onstage **CROWD** approach with coins, grabbing newspapers, pushing and shoving **MICKEY** and themselves offstage. One **MAN** in the crowd drops his crutch and keeps moving. **FOSWELL** picks up the crutch and taps one of the **MEN** on the back.)*

FOSWELL. Excuse me, sir.

FIRST MAN (MAN #3). Yes, what is it?

FOSWELL. I was wondering if this crutch –

FIRST MAN (MAN #3). *(He sees the crutch)* Crutch? Oh. You poor lad. I'm so sorry.

*(He drops some coins in **FOSWELL**'s cup, and exits. **FOSWELL**, alone onstage, is stunned. **MICKEY** returns, all his papers gone, counting coins. A **SECOND MAN** enters, going in the opposite direction.)*

FOSWELL. Excuse me, sir, but are you looking for this?

*(The **MAN** turns.)*

SECOND MAN (MAN #2). Oh, what a pity. Well, good luck, son.

*(He drops more coins into **FOSWELL**'s cup and exits.)*

MICKEY. Hunter knew his onions. We both shoulda listened earlier.

FOSWELL. But Mickey, I can't keep –

MICKEY. Let's get outta here before that mob finds out we're not at war.

FOSWELL. Mickey, it's not right. I can walk without a crutch!

MICKEY. Well, praise the Lord! And tomorrow, Foswell, add an eyepatch!

*(**FOSWELL** figures it out and happily hobbles off, crutch under his arm.)*

(blackout)

Scene Eleven

(*SETTING:* **SNOBDEN**'s *store.*)

(*TIME:* *Late afternoon.*)

(*AT RISE:* **HIGGINS** *is lazily placing boxes in a display case.* **CHAPIN** *is studying an inventory list.* **DICK** *enters the store. He has pamphlets with him and lesson books, which he puts on the counter.*)

DICK. You're gonna love this, Mr. Chapin.

CHAPIN. Where have you been?!

(**SNOBDEN** *enters from his office.*)

DICK. I was passin' City Hall, and I went to see some old customers of mine in the Building Codes and Zoning Department.

CHAPIN. Building Codes and – That's what I was planning to do!

SNOBDEN. (*glancing over the pamphlets*) You thought of it, but he's done it. This is exactly the information I need for the planned expansion. Very enterprising, Hunter. I think it's time you had the key. Chapin, give it to him.

CHAPIN. But he's the office boy.

SNOBDEN. I think he's proven he's a Snobden man. Give him the key.

CHAPIN. As you say, sir.

(*He gives* **DICK** *the key.*)

SNOBDEN. I have the other one, Dick. You open the shop each day and close it each evening. Now, you deserve a little something for the bank account of yours.

(*He discovers he has no cash in his pockets.*)

Come into my office.

(*Crossing to his office door,* **SNOBDEN** *sees* **HIGGINS**, *who is dozing at the counter.*)

Higgins!

(**SNOBDEN** *and* **DICK** *exit.* **HIGGINS** *and* **CHAPIN** *glare at each other.*)

Song - *A HARDWORKING BOY*

CHAPIN.
> A HARDWORKING BOY –
> A GENUINE JOY –
> DEVOTED AND LOYAL –
> I HATE HIM!

HIGGINS.
> NOT LAZY OR SLY –
> AND WON'T TELL A LIE –
> HE'S NOTHING LIKE I AM –
> I HATE HIM!

CHAPIN.
> A LAD OF SENSITIVITY
> WHO KNOWS WHAT YOU ARE FEELING –

HIGGINS.
> HE'S UTTERLY INCAPABLE OF
> SORDID DOUBLE-DEALING –

CHAPIN.
> WITH ONE DISTURBING
> FEATURE THAT I FIND IS MOST REVEALING –

CHAPIN & HIGGINS.
> NO STEALING! WE HATE HIM!

SNOBDEN. *(offstage) (laugh)* Good for you, Hunter!

(**DICK** *laughs too.*)

HIGGINS.
> THAT BOY IS A THREAT –

CHAPIN.
> HE'S SNOBDEN'S NEW PET –

HIGGINS.
> I NEVER CAN GET
> HIM IN DUTCH!

CHAPIN.
>HE MEETS MY EYE
>WITH HEAD HELD HIGH
>AND WON'T TALK BACK NO MATTER HOW I
>BERATE HIM –
>I HATE HIM
>SO MUCH!

>*(**DICK** re-enters, humming happily. As the two watch him closely, he gathers his books from the counter, taking time to dust it. By habit, **HIGGINS** has begun to mop the floor. **DICK** approaches.)*

DICK. Mr. Higgins you shouldn't be doing that, let me.

>*(**DICK** pries the mop from **HIGGINS**' grasp, picks up the pail and exits into the stockroom.)*

HIGGINS. *(staring after him)*
>I THINK WE AGREE
>THAT IF HE COULD BE
>A BIT MORE LIKE WE ARE,
>WE'D LOVE HIM –

CHAPIN.
>I SEE MORE AND MORE
>THERE'S TROUBLE IN STORE
>UNLESS OUT THE DOOR
>WE CAN SHOVE HIM –

HIGGINS.
>THE DAY THAT HE WALKED IN THE PLACE,
>WE'RE GONNA MAKE HIM RUE IT –

CHAPIN.
>A WICKED LITTLE PLOT IS WHAT WE NEED
>AND WE CAN BREW IT –

BOTH.
>WHEN THERE ARE BRAINS
>LIKE YOURS AND MINE,
>THERE'S REALLY NOTHING TO IT –
>WE'LL DO IT!
>WE HATE HIM!

HIGGINS.
>THAT TRUSTWORTHY AIR –

CHAPIN.
>THAT DRESSING WITH CARE –

HIGGINS.
>AND WHAT'S MOST UNFAIR,
>HE CAN'T SPELL!

BOTH. *(choking a nearby upturned broom)*
>WE'D BE SO GLAD TO TAKE THIS LAD
>AND JUST FOR FUN COMPLETELY ERADICATE HIM –
>WE HATE HIM...

>*(**DICK** re-enters suddenly, stares at them in puzzlement, shrugs, begins to mop...)*

HIGGINS & CHAPIN. *(very quietly to each other)*
>LIKE HELL!

>*(**HIGGINS** exits to the stockroom. **DICK** sets down the mop and pail, crosses to a ladder on the opposite side of the store from **CHAPIN**, climbs up and begins cleaning a high shelf.)*

>*(**ALLEN CARLISLE** and his son, **ROB**, enter the store.)*

CHAPIN. Mr. Carlisle! Welcome to Snobden's. May I help you?

CARLISLE. Thank you, Mr. Chapin. Would you make a new suit for my son? He needs one for the fall.

CHAPIN. Of course. *(bending down for a closer look)* What a pleasant little boy.

CARLISLE. Rob, this is Mr. Chapin.

ROB. Hello.

>*(shakes hands)*

CHAPIN. Rob, is it? Come with me and we'll get you measured. Why don't you look around, Mr. Carlisle? We have some very good buys at the moment.

CARLISLE. I will. Thank you.

>*(**CHAPIN** and **ROB** exit into the stockroom.)*

DICK. *(from the ladder)* Hello, Mr. Carlisle.

CARLISLE. Ah, Dick. Nice to see you again. I've kept my eye on your account. I see it's growing.

DICK. *(stepping down from the ladder)* Yeah, by leaps and crawls.

CARLISLE. You've started, that's the point. Some never do.

DICK. I'm learning' to read.

CARLISLE. Good!

(LUKE GERRISH enters the store. DICK reacts.)

DICK. Just a moment, sir.

CARLISLE. I'll just have a look around.

(He wanders off.)

DICK. *(to GERRISH)* You shouldn't come here.

GERRISH. Where should I come then? You ain't mentioned where you live.

DICK. I'm not givin' you nothin'.

GERRISH. I'm your stepfather. Legal. I waited till you got settled here. You ain't givin' me the brush, kid.

(He grabs him.)

CARLISLE. *(in earshot, has overheard)* Dick, can you help me with this?

DICK. Yes, Mr. Carlisle.

CARLISLE. *(approaching)* I don't mean to interrupt.

DICK. Oh. *(an awkward moment)* This is Luke Gerrish.

(to GERRISH)

Mr. Carlisle. One of our regular customers.

CARLISLE. How do you do?

GERRISH. Likewise.

DICK. Luke's my stepfather. I've seen him twice in three years. He's been out of town.

CARLISLE. *(to DICK)* Do you support yourself in this job?

DICK. Well, I ain't got no maiden aunt who left me her fortune.

CARLISLE. *(to* **GERRISH***)* And you, sir. You're strong and able-bodied. You must earn your own living.

GERRISH. I can't get work.

CARLISLE. A wagon of coal is being delivered to my house in an hour. Go up there and I'll give you the job of putting it in the cellar and pay you one dollar. Here's my card. What do you say?

GERRISH. I've had nothin' to eat today, sir. I wouldn't have the strength for that job. If you'll give me a quarter, I'll get a little supper and then go right to it.

CARLISLE. I will leave orders in the kitchen that you are to have supper. So – done?

GERRISH. Yes. All right. Done. You may expect me. Thank you.

(One last look at **DICK** *and he exits.)*

DICK. He won't come.

CARLISLE. No, I don't think he will.

*(***ROB** *and* **CHAPIN** *re-enter.)*

Ah, there you are, Rob. I'd like you to meet Richard Hunter.

(Music begins.)

ROB. How do you do?

DICK. Hello, Rob.

*(***DICK** *sees* **CHAPIN** *signaling him.)*

Excuse me, I have to finish my work.

*(***DICK** *begins moving boxes from one side of the store to the other.* **ROB** *watches him as* **CARLISLE** *watches both.)*

CHAPIN. Will you be in soon to select a fabric for Rob's suit?

CARLISLE. What? Oh, yes. After the holiday. I like the boy, don't you?

CHAPIN. Oh, yes. He's a treasure.

CARLISLE. Rob seems to like him too.

CHAPIN. That's nice. Everybody likes everybody.

(During the above **CARLISLE** *and* **CHAPIN** *exchange, choreographed to the musical duet,* **ROB** *has crossed the stage and has picked up a box directly behind* **DICK**. **DICK** *turns.* **ROB** *is standing there and hands the box to* **DICK**. **DICK** *smiles, takes it, crosses for two more.* **ROB** *follows and picks up the last of them, following* **DICK** *as before and presenting him with the box.* **DICK** *then moves to a display case and begins to polish the brass fixtures with a style that reminds us of his flair with a shoeshine rag.* **ROB** *follows, watching him work.* **DICK** *rips the cloth in two and gives* **ROB** *half. The two boys continue to shine and polish together.* **CARLISLE**, *who has seen it all, crosses to* **DICK**.)

CARLISLE. *(continuing)* Dick, would you consider coming up each evening to spend some time with Rob?

DICK. Well, I do my readin' and writin' lessons most every night.

CARLISLE. Just for company. My work keeps me out much of the time, and you seem to get along well together. I'll pay you what you earn here.

ROB. He said he's got lessons to do.

DICK. Now hold on, Rob. I could do mine while you're doin' yours. I mean eight dollars a week. That's a lot! Would it be OK with you?

ROB. I don't mind.

CARLISLE. Fine, fine! Why don't you join us on the fourth for the big goings-on in Union Square.

DICK. Well, I told my friend – aw, he won't mind.

(a beat)

I'd love to!

CARLISLE. Good! Even better, start your new job right now.

DICK. I'm not quite finished here.

CARLISLE. It's almost six.

(to **CHAPIN***)*

Surely, Mr. Chapin, you won't mind the boy leaving a few minutes early. This is a special weekend.

CHAPIN. If it will please you – why not?

(**DICK** *takes off the* **SNOBDEN** *jacket, and puts on his own.*)

CARLISLE. Thank you. I do hope you'll have a memorable holiday. With your family, I suppose?

CHAPIN. That's correct, sir. My dear sister and I have bought some fireworks for my nephew with which we will be tinkering in our own little garden.

CARLISLE. Do be careful. You wouldn't want a rocket carrying the boy off to Mars.

CHAPIN. Certainly not!

(*He opens the door for them, as* **DICK** *passes.*)

Do they have rockets that do that?

(**CARLISLE** *and* **ROB** *exit to the street outside the store with* **DICK** *as the set begins to change.*)

ROB. Look, Dick – a new cap for the centennial. What exactly is that?

CARLISLE. It's a party for the country's hundredth birthday. A few speeches and lots of talk about where we came from.

ROB. We came from 29th Street.

CARLISLE. No, long before that. Our people. Dick's people. Before we were us.

LOOK HOW FAR WE'VE COME

CARLISLE. (*continuing*)
STARTING OUT AS NO ONE,
AS SUBJECTS OF A KING –
WE LOOKED AROUND
AND SOON WE FOUND
THAT KINGS DON'T MEAN A THING –

LIVING LIFE AS NO ONE
WAS ONCE ALL RIGHT FOR SOME,
BUT LOOK HOW FAR WE'VE COME!

(*As the music continues, other voices join as the stage is transformed and the lights come up to a brighter, sunnier level and we are in Union Square on the Fourth of July, 1876.*)

Scene Twelve

(*SETTING: Union Square, Fourth of July. Flags, posters of President Grant and Uncle Sam, a telescope, a lung capacity tester, root beer stand, weight machine and various artifacts of 1876 and the Centennial.*)

(*TIME: Segue from previous scene.*)

(*AT RISE:* **CARLISLE**, **DICK** *and* **ROB** *are in the midst of the celebration in progress. Out of the crowd appear* **MRS. MOONEY** *and* **MRS. McHUGH**, *waving little souvenir flags.*)

Song - LOOK HOW FAR WE'VE COME (cont'd)

CROWD. (*louder now*)
CROSSED A LOT OF OCEANS
AND SHED A LOT OF TEARS –
THROUGH TIME AND TIDE,
WE LIVED AND DIED
ACROSS A LOT OF YEARS –
MADE THIS LAND A PROMISE
AND GAVE THIS LAND A NAME –
AND LOOK HOW FAR WE CAME!

CARLISLE.
EVERY DAY'S A NEW BEGINNING,
EVERY DAY'S A RACE –
EVERY DAY'S A DOOR THAT MIGHT GET
SLAMMED RIGHT IN YOUR FACE –

LOTS OF GUTS IS WHAT IT TAKES
TO GET FROM THERE TO HERE –

CARLISLE & CHORUS.
ANYONE WHO DOES DESERVES
A BANNER AND A CHEER! –

SNOBDEN.
IN THAT BOSTON HARBOR
THEY THREW A LOT OF TEA –

AND THROUGH US FLOWS
THE BLOOD OF THOSE
AMERICANS TO BE!

MOONEY & McHUGH.
STARTING OUT IN BOSTON,
THE ROAD IS MIGHTY LONG,

SNOBDEN & CARLISLE.
BUT WE'RE STILL GOING STRONG!

ALL.
STILL GOING GOOD AND STRONG!

(**FOSWELL** *enters, limping on his crutch, wearing an eye patch and a slightly bloody bandage. He passes* **MOONEY** *and* **McHUGH.**)

MOONEY. Mr. Foswell! Were you hit by a trolley?!

FOSWELL. I'm working, Mrs. Mooney.

McHUGH. Is it Halloween?

MOONEY. *(to* **FOSWELL***)* Where's Richard? He said he'd be with you.

FOSWELL. Did he? Well, he's not. He's in the park somewhere with his new family.

MOONEY. Oh, dear. Well, if you're on your own, join Mary McHugh and me.

McHUGH. Yes, dear, whoever you are, do!

FOSWELL. I was going to work.

MOONEY. Not today.

FOSWELL. That's right. So thank you, ladies. And we'll have a us a fine time!

McHUGH. Oh, we will.

MOONEY. Won't we though.

ALL.
WE ALL STARTED SOMEWHERE,
BUT SOMEWHERE ISN'T HERE –
WE LOOKED AROUND
AT WHAT WE'VE FOUND
AND WHAT WE'VE FOUND IS CLEAR:

SOMEWHERE'S THE BEGINNING

THAT WE ALL STARTED FROM,
AND LOOK HOW FAR WE'VE COME!
HOW VERY FAR WE'VE COME!

*(The music suspends without a finish as **GERRISH** and **STACIA** are seen.)*

STACIA. Oh, Luke. A day off!

GERRISH. Yeah, lovely.

*(He spots **DICK**, **CARLISLE** and **ROB**.)*

Well, that's a surprise. Hunter and that banker. And he's got a kid with him.

*(**MICKEY MAGUIRE** approaches a **MAN** and a **WOMAN**, center stage. **GERRISH** sees this too.)*

MICKEY. Ain't it one of the finest fourths you've ever seen?

*(He "trips" into the **WOMAN** (**MRS. HALLIWELL**), bumping her and sending her slightly reeling. She is assisted by others around her, finding her a seat, fanning her, etc.)*

Oh, excuse me, ma'am. My fault.

*(**MICKEY** has stolen a small purse which she had been carrying attached to her waist. He moves past **GERRISH**, who stops him.)*

GERRISH. I caught your act, kid. Not bad.

*(He looks back at **DICK** and his group.)*

I got an idea. I want to talk to you.

STACIA. Not today! Today is for us.

GERRISH. Get some lemonade. I'll find you – just stay in the park.

*(back to **MICKEY**)*

Yeah, I want to talk to you.

(They exit.)

ROB. Can we have a rootbeer, father?

CARLISLE. You have one.

(He reaches into his pocket.)

DICK. *(to* **CARLISLE***)* You paid for the lunch. I'll stand treat for the rootbeer.

*(***DICK** *and* **ROB** *head for the rootbeer stand as a recovered* **MRS. HALLIWELL** *approaches* **CARLISLE**. *Somewhere in the distance a waltz begins. Nearby, couples are dancing.)*

HALLIWELL (WOMAN #4). Allen, of course you're here. Isn't it fun to mix with the peasants?

CARLISLE. Gail, you are the most attractive snob I know.

HALLIWELL. They're playing a waltz, Allen. And you know how I adore waltzing with you. Would you?

CARLISLE. I'd love to, since you taught me how. But I'm here with Rob and his friend.

*(***ROB** *and* **DICK** *return with their rootbeers.)*

HALLIWELL. Darling Rob, won't you lend me your handsome father for just one waltz?

ROB. All right. If it's a short one.

HALLIWELL. Bless you, darling. I won't keep him long.

CARLISLE. Keep an eye on him, will you, Dick.

DICK. Yes, sir.

*(***CARLISLE** *and* **MRS. HALLIWELL** *move into crowd and dance.* **ROB** *hands his rootbeer to* **DICK**.*)*

ROB. Here's your change.

(sips his)

DICK. I'm getting awful used to this high life. Your life and mine are so different.

ROB. *(pause)* Is your mother dead?

DICK. What?! Yes, she is.

ROB. My father told me. So is mine.

DICK. I know.

ROB. I'm not lonely, but I remember her. I'll always remember her. So you see? We do have something the same.

DICK. I guess we do.

(to the melody of the distant waltz)

EVERYONE'S FROM SOMEWHERE,
SOME CORNER OF THE EARTH –
WE'VE LEFT BEHIND THOSE TIES THAT BIND
AND NOW WE KNOW OUR WORTH!

ROB.

EVERYONE'S FROM SOMEWHERE –

DICK.

SO PLAY THAT FIFE AND DRUM

BOTH.

TO MARK HOW FAR WE'VE COME!

(They clink glasses in a toast to that. The waltz ends. **HALLIWELL** *and* **CARLISLE** *finish their dance,* **STACIA** *is sitting alone. A* **MAN** *approaches her.)*

MAN (MAN #1). Are you on your own, sister? 'Cause I am. And I'd like not to be.

STACIA. No. I'm waiting for someone.

MAN. Aren't we all?

STACIA. I said, "No!"

CARLISLE. *(overhears)* You heard the lady. On your way.

MAN. Who are you? Her white knight?

CARLISLE. I said, "Move!"

MAN. And a happy fourth to you, too.

(He goes.)

STACIA. *(to* **CARLISLE***)* Thank you.

CARLISLE. The holiday brings out some beauts, doesn't it?

STACIA. It does.

HALLIWELL. *(who has been nearby)* What a lovely dress, dear.

STACIA. Thank you. I made it myself.

HALLIWELL. I can use a good seamstress.

CARLISLE. I don't think the young lady is in the park looking for work.

HALLIWELL. Isn't she?

CARLISLE. Gail!

STACIA. Thank you for your help. I should be going.

CARLISLE. No, I think Mrs. Halliwell should be going. She just stopped by for a dance, and now she's had it.

HALLIWELL. I spy Jason Pomeroy over there. He's usually good for six tickets to my charity supper and I mustn't let him slip away. Thank you for the waltz, Allen. Miss. Ta ta.

(She goes as music begins again. A bright gallop, and the dancing resumes.)

CARLISLE. *(to STACIA)* Now we're both on our own.

STACIA. It seems so.

CARLISLE. Would you allow me to escort you to the center stand? It's above the crowd and you'll be better able to watch for your friend.

STACIA. I'd like that.

(GERRISH enters the area with MICKEY. He sees CARLISLE and STACIA leaving.)

CARLISLE. *(to STACIA)* You see? Things have a way of working out.

(He offers her his arm, and she takes it. They merge with the crowd.)

GERRISH. *(to MICKEY)* You sure you can do this?

MICKEY. Mister, for a hundred bucks I'll do anything.

GERRISH. *(He looks after CARLISLE and STACIA.)* You just do what I told you. Understand?

MICKEY. Sure, Mister.

GERRISH. *(He turns to DICK and ROB, stage left.)* Now!

(MICKEY and GERRISH merge with the crowd. DICK lifts his rootbeer. ROB lifts his too and spills a little.)

DICK. Watch it! Root beer and linen suits don't like each other much.

(He takes out his handkerchief, the fancy one from the store, and starts to clean ROB's jacket. ROB takes the

handkerchief, does it himself and puts the handkerchief in his pocket. **DICK** *takes out his change purse to put some change away.* **MICKEY** *appears.)*

MICKEY. Now if I only had a nickel, I could have some rootbeer.

DICK. I don't like loans, Mick. A gift. Even for "the world owes me a livin'" you. I'm willin' to share.

(He opens the change purse, **MICKEY** *grabs it.)*

MICKEY. Well, well – look at all that money. A little nickel ain't sharin'. It's charity. And what's this? A bankbook? Well, La De Da!

(He dances around **DICK**, *poking in the purse.)*

DICK. That's none of your business. Hand it over!

(makes a grab for it)

MICKEY. You want it back? You'll have to catch me then, won't you?

(He wheels and runs. The music ends and the dancers politely applaud.)

DICK. Mickey!

(...and **DICK** *follows him off, right.)*

ROB. Dick! Dick!

*(***ROB** *doesn't know what to do. He decides to follow* **DICK** *and starts off. But* **GERRISH**, *who has been watching nearby, moves in.)*

GERRISH. What is it, little fella? What happened?

ROB. A man just stole my friend's money!

GERRISH. Well then, I'll help you. Let's you and me find a copper.

ROB. Yes. Thank you very much.

*(***GERRISH** *takes* **ROB**'s *hand and starts to lead him off.)*

GERRISH. I saw one standing right over there.

ROB. Wait! I'm not supposed to go anywhere with strangers.

GERRISH. We won't be strangers long, son. You and me are gonna be spendin' some time together!

*(He lunges for **ROB** and picks him up as...)*

ROB. No! Help! Dick! Anybody!

*(At the precise moment **ROB** begins to scream, there is an explosive, loud fanfare of music and a blinding burst of bright light as all eyes in the **CROWD** look upward, fixed on the fireworks display overhead. As **GERRISH** runs off with the struggling boy, **ROB**'s cap falls to the ground.)*

ALL. *(almost surreal, in slow motion)*
EVERYONE FROM FROM EAST TO WEST
FROM SUNNY SOUTH TO NORTH –
HERE ON OUR CENTENNIAL,
THIS GRAND JULY THE FOURTH –

HERE ON OUR CENTENNIAL
WE'RE GONNA MAKE THINGS HUM –
YOU WON'T RECOGNIZE US
IN THE HUNDRED YEARS TO COME!

*(**DICK** re-enters, out of breath, with his coin purse. He looks about for **ROB** and becomes increasingly disturbed as he sees no sign of him anywhere. In the distance we see **GERRISH** carrying off the screaming boy, not heard over the noise.)*

(back to real time, in tempo)

NOW AND THEN WE STUMBLE
AND NOW AND THEN WE FALL –
WE LOSE OUR WAY
AND GO ASTRAY
AND SEE NO PATH AT ALL –

*(As the number builds to its climax, **DICK** finds Rob's cap on the ground. He picks it up, looks at it, looks off right, then left. The music and fireworks continue.)*

THEN WE LOOK BEHIND US
AND, LO, WE'RE NOT SO DUMB
FOR LOOK HOW FAR WE'VE COME!
HOW VERY FAR WE'VE COME!

(After the last note of music, in the final seconds, the **CROWD** *erupts in a monumental cheer, madly waving its banners, flags and posters while* **DICK** *stands silently, center stage, looking at the cap as...)*

(curtain)

End of Act One

ACT II

Scene One

(SETTING: Limbo)

(TIME: Later that day.)

*(AT RISE: The stage is filled with people of the neighborhood. Throughout, there is constant sense of human traffic, frantically crossing from all directions. Eventually, **DICK** and **CARLISLE** are in front, each with a separate group.)*

Song - *FIND THAT BOY!*

DICK.
>FRIENDS AND NEIGHBORS!
>I KNOW WE CAN FIND HIM –
>WE'RE NOT FAR BEHIND HIM –
>IF WE'RE SMART!

CARLISLE.
>FRIENDS AND NEIGHBORS!
>KEEP A CAREFUL LOOK OUT –
>SEARCH EACH LITTLE NOOK OUT –
>MAKE A START!

ENSEMBLE.
>UPTOWN, DOWNTOWN,
>BATTERY TO WALL STREET –
>THROUGH EACH BIG AND SMALL STREET –
>WE'LL PURSUE!

>WE'LL UNEARTH HIM,
>THOUGH HE MAY BE WAY OFF –
>WE WON'T TAKE A DAY OFF
>TILL WE DO!

CARLISLE.
> FIND HIM!

ENSEMBLE SOLO #1 (WOMAN #3).
> WE'LL HAVE HIM BACK WITH MISTER CARLISLE QUICK!

DICK.
> FIND HIM!

ENSEMBLE SOLO #2 (MAN #3).
> IT'S KNOWING WHERE TO LOOK THAT DOES THE TRICK!

ENSEMBLE.
> FIND HIM!

CARLISLE.
> I NEVER SHOULD HAVE LEFT HIM THERE LIKE THAT!

ENSEMBLE.
> (WE'LL) FIND HIM!

DICK.
> TO SEE HIS CAP JUST LYING THERE LIKE THAT!

ENSEMBLE.
> WHEN WE'VE DONE IT,
> WHAT A FUSS AND BOTHER –
> SEE THE HAPPY FATHER
> WEEP FOR JOY!

DICK, CARLISLE & ALL.
> FRIENDS AND NEIGHBORS!
> EVERYBODY FAN OUT –
> AND TO MAKE IT PAN OUT
> FIND THAT BOY!

*(The **CROWD** moves off in different directions.)*

DICK. *(sees **CARLISLE**)* Mr. Carlisle! I've got everyone I know out working on it.

CARLISLE. Never mind that. I left him in your care. What was in that purse that made you leave him there? Two dollars? I'd have given you that. Two dollars – and I've lost my son!

DICK. We'll get him back.

CARLISLE. You don't know that!

(He turns away.)

MICKEY. *(with **GERRISH**, in another part of the street)* Hey, Gerrish, where's my hundred bucks?

GERRISH. You'll get your money when the deal is complete.

MICKEY. You said I'd have it today.

GERRISH. Now scram. We shouldn't be seen together. And if anyone asks if you know me – you don't. Clear?

MICKEY. Yeah, it's clear.

> THEY'LL NEVER
> FIND HIM!

GERRISH.

> HIS FATHER'S VERY RICH, HE'LL PAY FOR SURE!

(They part, and both exit.)

DICK.

> FIND HIM!

ENSEMBLE SOLO #4 (WOMAN #4, WOMAN #2).

> KIDS ARE NEVER KIDNAPPED WHEN THEY'RE POOR!

CARLISLE & DICK.

> FIND HIM!

ENSEMBLE SOLO #5 (MAN #2, WOMAN #1).

> WE'LL KEEP ON LOOKING MORNING, NIGHT AND NOON!

CARLISLE & DICK.

> FIND HIM!

ENSEMBLE SOLO #6 (MAN #3, MAN #1).

> WE'LL START BY SEARCHING EVERY LAST SALOON!

ENSEMBLE.

> WHEN WE FREE HIM,
> WHAT A CELEBRATION –
> BIG AS ALL CREATION –
> WE'LL ENJOY –

DICK & CARLISLE.

> EVERYBODY!
> GLAD WE ALL AGREE NOW –
> SAY IT AFTER ME NOW –

ALL.

> FIND THAT BOY!
> *(They scatter. Blackout.)*

Scene Two

(SETTING: Snobden's Store.)

(TIME: Two days later. Very early morning.)

(AT RISE: **HIGGINS** *is pacing, mumbling to himself.* **CHAPIN** *arrives, bangs on the door.* **HIGGINS** *jumps.)*

HIGGINS. *(muttering, scratching)* Who is it? Oh my God.

(opens door)

CHAPIN. *(enters)* We're late. We have only minutes until they get here. Did I wake you?

HIGGINS. You didn't wake me because I wasn't asleep. All night! There were dogs howling and cats screaming at each other. I was terrified.

CHAPIN. Well, it's morning now. Calm yourself.

HIGGINS. I can't! Have you ever been locked in a shop all night long?!

CHAPIN. You had to be locked in and you know it. Hunter has the only key now – other than Snobden's.

HIGGINS. But to hide me in an overcoat in the stockroom in summer! I nearly suffocated before you all left last night.

CHAPIN. Nearly doesn't count.

HIGGINS. How would you like to be dead?

CHAPIN. Be quiet, Higgins. All this friction will disappear once Hunter is gone.

(He has started to open drawers and throw papers in the air.)

Now hop to it.

HIGGINS. I can't.

CHAPIN. Can't?? That's become your favorite word. I won't have it!

HIGGINS. Snobden will feel sorry for Hunter and accuse us. Like he always does. Really, I am very close to the edge.

CHAPIN. I think you've gone OVER the edge. Accuse us? When it looks like Hunter was so clearly negligent? Not to mention where he went last night after he left here. I'm no fool, Higgins. On occasion, I've pretended to take him into my confidence on some trivial matter just so that, on occasion, he would take me into his. I know plenty about him.

HIGGINS. But what if we're caught?

CHAPIN. How can you be caught?

HIGGINS. Me?? What about you??

CHAPIN. I'm not involved. I was at home last night, reading "David Copperfield." But fear not Higgins, if need be, I shall stand behind you right up to the prison gate.

HIGGINS. I want my mother.

CHAPIN. I told Hunter you'd left last night. He thinks he was the last one out.

HIGGINS. If Snobden questions me, I'll have to lie. I'll be a perjurer, a criminal. Those are not good credentials!

CHAPIN. Get hold of yourself, boy. We have work to do.

(He opens another drawer, flings things about.)

HIGGINS. No! I was a good person once. My mother loved me. I had friends. I used to smile once in a while. They'd ask "How are you, Herbert?" or "Want to have lunch?" But then I came here and became Higgins. Oh God, I made a wrong turn somewhere – the day I saw the sign that read "Stock Boy Wanted," turned left, and came through that door.

CHAPIN. But you'll join me?

HIGGINS. Oh, yes.

CHAPIN. Good.

Song - A HARDWORKING BOY (Reprise)

HIGGINS.
THE LORD ONLY KNOWS
THAT BOY HAS HIS WOES –
HE'S SUFFERED SUCH BLOWS –
I – STILL HATE HIM!

(During the course of the song, they shred paper, overturn furniture, do battle with and defeat a mannequin, etc.)

CHAPIN.

I'VE THOUGHT OF A PLAN
AND SOON AS WE CAN
WE'LL TOTALLY ANN-
I-HI-LATE HIM!

HIGGINS.

ATTENTIVE AND EFFICIENT,
EVERY CUSTOMER AGREES HE
IS EAGER AND INTELLIGENT
WITH MANNER BRIGHT AND BREEZY –

CHAPIN.

SO HOW CAN WE DESTROY THIS CHARMING LAD
AND NOT FEEL QUEASY?

BOTH.

IT'S EASY –
WE HATE HIM!

IT'S REALLY NO TRICK
TO GET RID OF DICK –
FOR SOON WE WILL THICKEN
THE PLOT!

AND HAPPILY
WE BOTH AGREE
IT'S GONNA BE A PLEASURE WHEN WE
DEFLATE HIM –
WE HATE HIM

(to a whisper)

A LOT!

(They carefully sneak out of the shop and close the door behind them. Immediately **SNOBDEN** *appears on the street, as does* **DICK**, *coming from another direction.)*

SNOBDEN. Ah, good morning. Any news?

DICK. No. I've got half the town out looking for him. It's two days and not even a ransom note.

SNOBDEN. I know how you feel. But the best cure for melancholy is hard work.

(They are at the door. **DICK**, *trying his key, finds the door unlocked.)*

DICK. Oh, jeez! The door was open.

SNOBDEN. Open? Open! I don't understand. Was it broken?

(He walks into the shop.)

We've been robbed!

*(***CHAPIN*** and ***HIGGINS*** *appear, heads first, at the open door)*

DICK. *(anxiously looking around)* I don't think anything's been taken. They just wanted to mess up the place.

SNOBDEN. "Just!" What do you mean, "just?"

*(***SNOBDEN*** *opens cash register, takes out a few bills to indicate contents are still there.)*

CHAPIN. *(peering around the store in pretend shock)* Mr. Snobden. I don't know what to say.

SNOBDEN. There's nothing to say. What's at the bottom of this?

HIGGINS. *(suddenly remembering his part)* I must check the stock room! Oh, I pray it's all right.

(He runs into the stock room.)

SNOBDEN. *(to* **DICK***)* Were you the last one out last night?

DICK. Yes, of course I was.

SNOBDEN. Didn't you lock the door?

DICK. I always lock the door.

SNOBDEN. Did you lock it last night!?

DICK. Yes!

CHAPIN. Now, now, Mr. Snobden. Dick's only had the key a few days. Perhaps it hasn't become ritual to him yet, as it had been to me. After all, sir, I'd been doing it for so long – and he's been under a terrible strain.

DICK. I remember locking the door!

CHAPIN. I have tried to teach you not to rush about so. Do you remember, last night, why you were in such a hurry to leave the shop?

DICK. That had nothing to do with it!

CHAPIN. I know the guilt with which you've been living since your negligence with that poor little Carlisle boy. But to neglect your duties in order to be punctual at – a poker game!

SNOBDEN. What's this? What's this?

DICK. That was a confidence! I was only going there because if I could get information anywhere about Rob, I could get it there.

CHAPIN. After all, with a father just free of prison, and you associated with a front-page crime, I hardly think you –

SNOBDEN. Do you play poker?

DICK. *(ignoring* **SNOBDEN**, *addressing* **CHAPIN***)* What do you mean "associated with?" I'm not a suspect!

CHAPIN. *(under his breath)* The *New York Herald* thinks you are.

SNOBDEN. Answer me! Do you play poker?

DICK. Now and then. But I told you –

SNOBDEN. No. I told you! I warned you about gambling when I engaged you.

DICK. Mr. Snobden I'm sure I locked it.

CHAPIN. I'm sure you meant to lock it. With all you have on your mind, you were just distracted. I don't say you lie – we do trust you.

SNOBDEN. I'm not certain. One earns trust.

DICK. I thought I had earned it.

SNOBDEN. So did I. That's why this disappoints me so.

*(***HIGGINS*** re-appears from the stock room.)*

HIGGINS. It's a miracle. The stock room is untouched!

CHAPIN. A ray of light in the darkness. Thank you, Higgins.

DICK. *(thinking it through as he changes into the Snobden jacket from the coat rack)*

SNOBDEN. I had confidence in you, you know that. You'll be paid through the week.

DICK. You're – firing me?!

SNOBDEN. I have no choice. Believe me, I wish I did. I've grown fond of you, which makes this difficult, but I cannot allow that to influence me. My name is on this establishment. I made a mistake.

(He exits.)

CHAPIN. Be certain to leave your key.

(DICK angrily crosses to the coat rack and removes the SNOBDEN jacket and puts on his own. He puts the key on the counter as CHAPIN crosses to the cash register and takes out some bills.)

Mr. Snobden said you were to be paid through the week.

(He gives four dollars to DICK.)

CHAPIN. *(brings up the bootblack box from behind counter)* And don't forget this. It's your future.

(He gives it to him.)

HIGGINS. Wait!

(Pause…CHAPIN stares at HIGGINS.)

You forgot your lesson books.

(He gives them to DICK from a nearby shelf.)

I'm sorry – I would – I didn't –

CHAPIN. Higgins!

HIGGINS. I'm sorry for you, Hunter.

(DICK exits as the music of "SHINE" sadly underscores his entry into the street outside Snobden's.)

Song - SHINE (Reprise)

DICK. *(sadly, with irony)*
> A SHINE
> IS REALLY ALL THAT YOU NEED
> AND YOU WILL SEE
> THERE'LL BE
> A CHANGE IN YOUR LUCK –
>
> A SHINE
> AND YOU ARE BOUND TO SUCCEED
> AND BY TONIGHT
> YOU MIGHT BE...

(more agitated, to imaginary customer)

> HEY, MISTER!
> WANNA SHOESHINE?
> I'LL MAKE' EM LOOK LIKE NEW –
> A RICHARD HUNTER SHOESHINE!
> SEE, THAT'S WHAT I DO –

(quietly)

> I USED TO WAKE UP WISHIN'
> THAT ALL THE WORLD WAS MINE –
> BUT NOW MY LIFE'S AMBITION
> STARTS AND ENDS WITH...

(Lights fade as he exits.)

Scene Three

(SETTING: **STACIA***'s room.)*

(TIME: Later, the same day.)

(AT RISE: **GERRISH** *is staring out the window.* **ROB***'s finished dinner is on a tray.* **STACIA** *enters.* **GERRISH** *turns to her.)*

GERRISH. Where's the kid?

STACIA. He needed the bathroom. I locked him in. Luke, he's half-dressed, and the window is six inches wide. He's not going anywhere.

GERRISH. *(not angry, playful)* I finished the letter. I'll take it to Carlisle and by tomorrow we'll be rich.

STACIA. You're going too fast. A few surprises; a stepson, an ex-wife, and now this.

GERRISH. I did this for us. And you are as much a part of it as I am. Picking up the kid's father in the park, wandering off with him. That's not hearsay in the eyes of the law. I saw that happen.

STACIA. You told me you've been out looking for work.

GERRISH. Work? The kid's father offered me work. Delivering coal to his mansion for a dollar. I didn't plan this, but opportunity, Stacia. When she knocks at the door, you open it.

Song - ***FROM NOW ON***

GERRISH.
> WAIT AND SEE
> HOW LOVELY LIFE IS GOING TO BE –
> WE'LL BE TAKING IT EASY
> FROM NOW ON!
>
> IF YOU LIKE,
> I'LL TAKE YOU SAILING OFF ON A SHIP –
> DRINK CHAMPAGNE FROM YOUR SLIPPER
> FROM NOW ON!

GERRISH. *(cont.)*
>AND ALL MY SHIRTS WILL BE OF SILK –
>I'LL ONLY SMOKE HAVANA CIGARS –
>THINGS OF GOLD
>AND WEALTH UNTOLD
>FROM JUST ONE BOLD
>DISPLAY OF DARING!
>
>EVERYONE
>WILL POINT US OUT WHEREVER WE GO –
>PEOPLE SAYING WE'RE SO
>RESPECTABLE!
>
>A LIFE LIKE THAT FOREVER –
>NO OTHER KIND WILL EVER
>COME NOW
>FROM NOW ON!

STACIA.
>WAIT AND SEE
>JUST WHAT THE BITTER TRUTH OF IT IS:
>WE'LL BE TRAPPED IN A PRISON
>FROM NOW ON!
>
>SOON WE'LL KNOW
>JUST HOW IT FEELS TO LIVE ON THE RUN –
>SO AFRAID OF THE SUNLIGHT
>FROM NOW ON!
>
>A STRANGER'S GLANCE WILL BE A THREAT,
>A WHISPERED WORD WILL CAUSE US TO FLY –
>
>YEAR BY YEAR,
>THOUGH FAR OR NEAR,
>WE'LL KNOW A FEAR
>THAT NEVER FREES US!

GERRISH.	**STACIA.**
EVERYONE	EVERYONE
WILL POINT US OUT	WILL POINT US OUT
WHEREVER WE GO!	WHEREVER WE GO!
PEOPLE SAYING WE'RE SO RESPECTABLE!	NEVER TO BE RESPECTABLE!

BOTH.
> A LIFE LIKE THAT FOREVER
> NO OTHER KIND WILL EVER
> COME NOW
> FROM NOW ON!

> (**STACIA** *defiantly pulls away from* **GERRISH**'s *embrace.*)

GERRISH. *(angry, but controlled)* Go get the kid! I want the ring he wears to put in the letter.

> (*She goes.* **GERRISH** *paces. He takes a small gun from his pocket, tucks in into his trousers.* **STACIA** *returns with* **ROB**.)

> I'm gonna leave a note for your father tonight telling him what he has to do. Carlisle's uptown, I'll be a while.

> (*He is gone.*)

STACIA. Rob, you must be exhausted. You haven't slept. Why don't you try?

ROB. I sure wouldn't want him as a cousin.

STACIA. He's not my cousin.

ROB. I knew it! Well, who is he then to talk to you like that?

STACIA. He's my – Shhh. Go to sleep.

> (*He slides into bed. She covers him. She crosses the room. Then, lost in thought…*)

Song - MAYBE TODAY (Reprise)

> DREAMS CAN COME TRUE
> AND WISHES GET GRANTED
> MAYBE TODAY –

> MIRACLES TOO
> ARE WAITING TO HAPPEN,
> MAYBE TOMORROW –

> (*a knock at the door*)

MRS. McHUGH. *(offstage)* Stacia-Jane?

> (**McHUGH** *enters with armful of linen.*)
> Evenin', dear.

STACIA. Mrs. McHugh.

McHUGH. I just came with your fresh linen.

STACIA. I told you I'd come get them.

McHUGH. You've told me a lot, dear. Like Mr. Gerrish is your cousin.

(She picks up the handkerchief.)

What a pretty handkerchief!

STACIA. *(ushering her out)* Take it, Mrs. McHugh. Just go. You'll wake the boy.

McHUGH. Oh, the boy, of course! Your nephew. Your cousin! You have such an interesting family.

*(She leaves. **STACIA** is at the door, turns, see that **ROB** is awake.)*

ROB. I didn't say anything.

STACIA. No.

ROB. She could have helped us get out of here. You could help us get out of here.

STACIA. Stop that. I can't.

ROB. Don't be sad, Stacia. You don't need him.

STACIA. Shhh.

(She goes to Chinese lantern, lit and glowing.)

MAYBE TOMORROW
TURNS INTO NEVER –
I COULD WAIT A LIFETIME,
I COULD WAIT FOREVER –

*(The music becomes bolder now, growing to a grand crescendo until it suddenly breaks off. Silence. She turns toward **ROB**.)*

Rob, we're leaving. Get dressed.

(She turns quickly and blows out the lantern as the music comes up full and triumphant.)

(blackout)

Scene Four

*(**SETTING**: Wall Street.)*

*(**TIME**: Immediately following.)*

*(**AT RISE**: **MICKEY MAGUIRE** is putting things away in his shoe box. **DICK** runs on. He's angry.)*

MICKEY. Well, La De Da. Look who's come slummin' in the old neighborhood. I just heard you got fired from Snobden's for stealin' or something.

DICK. What do you know about that?!

MICKEY. I was just playin' around. It's not my fault you thought two dollars change was more important than lookin' after that kid.

DICK. I'm warning you, Mick. No more!

MICKEY. I am trembling! You wanna make something out of it?

DICK. You're damned right I do!

*(And **DICK** is on him, fists flying. They go at it until **FOSWELL** enters.)*

FOSWELL. Hey, cut that out!

*(He gets between them. **MICKEY** takes another swipe.)*

McGuire. Leave him alone!

MICKEY. Yeah. Why should I fuss myself over two back numbers like you? I don't need to fight. You got nothin' I want.

(He picks up his bootblack box,)

You didn't throw yours out. That's good. You're gonna need it.

(He exits.)

DICK. He's right, you know.

FOSWELL. I stopped by the store to check on you. Chapin couldn't contain himself, he was so happy to give me the news.

DICK. *(lost)* He's right.

FOSWELL. You've cut your hand.

DICK. Yeah, looks it.

FOSWELL. Have you got a handkerchief?

DICK. No.

FOSWELL. I do. *(takes it out)* What happened to your fancy one?

DICK. *(realizing it for the first time)* I don't know. I must have lost it.

(checks)

FOSWELL. Open your hand.

(He binds it, and ties it.)

Why did you brush me off for them on the Fourth? You stepped right over me. I get enough of that from customers. I don't need it from a friend. I seem to remember something about Hunter and Foswell.

DICK. You gotta give me time. I know lots of people but I ain't used to havin' friends.

FOSWELL. Don't say "ain't."

DICK. No more lessons! Anyway, "ain't" will work better with a bootblack box. You oughta try it.

FOSWELL. I don't need your help. It's not my life's work, but I'm doing all right now that I've got a character to play.

DICK. What character?

FOSWELL. Well, I'm sort of Tiny Tim. With a head wound. You taught me that. And if you'd asked me to be part of your big day in the Square, there might have been someone around to keep an eye on Rob Carlisle.

(He starts to leave.)

Keep your hand clean.

DICK. Where are you goin'?

FOSWELL. If everyone else is looking for him, I can too.

DICK. You'd do that for me?

*(**FOSWELL** just looks at him, exits. **DICK** paces. **GERRISH** enters.)*

GERRISH. You look like you lost a friend.

DICK. Yeah. A real friend.

GERRISH. I read about the kidnapping. The papers are playin' it up. I suppose that means you lost your job with Carlisle.

DICK. Snobden threw me out, too.

GERRISH. No...That don't seem right. We ain't rich. We ain't priv-i-ledged. Everyone's created equal, it says someplace. That's a crock. Me equal with Carlisle? You equal with his kid you're so worried about?

DICK. But Carlisle didn't start with anything. He made his own way.

GERRISH. Who knows what games he played to get there? It's up to you, son. You gotta change your ways. I am on to somethin' that will set me up for life. And I'm willing to share five hundred dollars of it – cash – for you – as soon as I get rid of the merchandise.

DICK. Five hundred dollars??!! Why me?

GERRISH. People like you. I've seen it. You meet people I can't meet. People on top. Doors open for you that close in my face. Wouldn't you like to be livin' in one of them fancy houses up on Washington Square?

DICK. Maybe I would. Hell, no maybe about it.

GERRISH. Well, good! Then we have lots to talk about. *(silence)* You'll have to be like me, kid, you really will. You'll have to be like me.

*(**GERRISH** takes out the ransom letter, looks at it, and exits, with a laugh. **DICK** stands a long moment.)*

Song - YES!

DICK.
I'LL HAVE TO BE LIKE YOU, GERRISH –
DO ALL THE THINGS YOU DO, GERRISH –
AND LIE AND CHEAT AND STEAL, GERRISH
TO LIVE JUST LIKE THE REAL GERRISH –

LOOKING IN A MIRROR, WILL I BE THERE
OR BE SEEING YOU, INSTEAD OF ME THERE?

*(A **MAN** enters. He sees **DICK**, and comes to him.)*

MAN (MAN #2). Hey kid, you busy? I need a shine.

DICK. What? Oh. Sure.

MAN. You're dressed kinda fancy for a bootblack.

DICK. Oh, these? They're just part of my act. They make people notice me, like you did, that's all.

(He starts the shine.)

DID I WANT TO MOVE OUT OF THAT BOX? YES –
DID I WANT A DOOR OF MINE THAT LOCKS? YES –
DID I WANT A FUTURE THAT WAS BETTER THAN MY PAST?
DID I DREAM THAT SOME DAY I'D BE OFF THE STREET AT LAST?

DID I WANT TO KEEP ON SHINING SHOES? NO! –
NEVER USE THE BRAINS THAT OTHERS USE? NO! –
DID I WANT TO REACH FOR STARS? I WILLINGLY CONFESS
YES! YES! YES!

(He finishes the shine.)

MAN. How much?

DICK. Just a nickel.

MAN. Here y'are.

*(The **MAN** takes out a change purse, pulls out loose papers, fishes for a nickel. A $10 bill falls to the ground but the **MAN** doesn't notice. **DICK** looks to the bill on the ground. **DICK** slowly picks up the $10. Maybe he hesitates a second, maybe not –)*

DICK. Hey, Mister. Mister! This is yours.

MAN. *(looks in his change purse)* What? Oh, God. Thanks!

(He takes it and leaves.)

DICK.

DO I WANT TO DO THE THINGS I SHOULD? YES –
WANT TO BE A MAN BOTH STRONG AND GOOD? YES –

IF MY PA COULD SEE ME NOW,
WOULD HE BE FEELING PROUD?
SAYING, "THAT'S MY BOY DOWN THERE!"
AND SHOUTING IT OUT LOUD?

DICK. *(cont.)*
>WILL I CREEP AND CRAWL RIGHT OUT OF SIGHT? NO! –
>WILL I TAKE A FALL AND THROW THE FIGHT? NO! –
>WILL I USE THE BEST IN ME AND NEVER ANY LESS?
>YES! YES! YES!
>
>GERRISH DOESN'T WASTE HIS TIME WITH RULES –
>WHO CARES FOR THOSE SILLY THINGS CALLED RULES?
>RULES ARE JUST FOR ANGELS OR FOR MULES –
>RULES ARE JUST FOR CHILDREN OR FOR FOOLS!
>
>IF I MUST GO BACK TO SHINING SHOES NOW –
>ALWAYS SHINING SHOES, NO MATTER WHOSE NOW –
>STARTING AT THE BOTTOM WITH WHATEVER COMES MY WAY –
>STARTING AT THE BOTTOM WILL I EVER BE O.K.?
>
>PULL YOURSELF TOGETHER, BOY AND SHUT UP!
>WHEN YOU'RE DOWN THERE'S NO DIRECTION BUT UP!
>
>WILL IT ALL TURN OUT ALL RIGHT?
>THAT'S ANYBODY'S GUESS –
>TRYING ONCE AGAIN MAY LEAD
>TO FAILURE OR SUCCESS –
>SHOULD I COUNT TO FIVE AND THEN
>START CLEANING UP THIS MESS?
>YES! YES! YES! YES! YES!

(blackout)

Scene Five

*(SETTING: The stoop in front of **MOONEY**'s boarding house.)*

(TIME: Later that evening.)

*(AT RISE: **MRS. MOONEY** is fanning herself with a cheap fan. She sips from a mug. Other mugs and pitcher on tray near her. **MRS. O'MALLEY** rushes in.)*

O'MALLEY (WOMAN #4). The others not here yet?

MOONEY. Not yet. Let's wait out here. How are the children, dear?

O'MALLEY. My mother was right. I should have been a nun.

*(**MRS. O'LEARY** and **MRS. CASSIDY** rush in.)*

O'LEARY (WOMAN #3). Finola May, we're late, and it wasn't our fault!

CASSIDY (WOMAN #1). The trolley was filled to the brim.

O'LEARY. With such riffraff. Nothin' but foreigners!

MOONEY. It's all right, ladies. Mary McHugh ain't here yet, as might be expected.

CASSIDY. It's only a poker game, Finola.

MOONEY. Poker is serious business, Maureen, and one of me few pleasures.

(She hands them mugs, and pours.)

And here's another one.

CASSIDY. Here's to our boyfriends and husbands.

THE OTHER THREE. May they never meet!

(They all drink, sigh.)

MOONEY. That is so good for the inner organs.

O'MALLEY. I remember the time I lost my great Aunt Moll on the trolley. I was so upset I had a load of this, and by the time I woke up, they'd found her!

O'LEARY. It lifts me right out of myself.

CASSIDY. It eases the soul.

MOONEY. That's right! It's God's own gift to mankind, ladies. Passed down from father to son, mother to daughter since the time of the Pharoahs of ancient Egypt. A recipe fit for kings!

Song - *A HANDFUL O' HOPS*

A HANDFUL O' HOPS,
A BIT O' THE BARLEY,
SOME WATER THAT'S COOL AND CLEAR –
IT'S EASY TO FIX IT,
A PADDLE TO MIX IT,
AND YOU'VE GOT YOURSELF SOME BEER!

O'LEARY.

A HANDFUL O' HOPS,

CASSIDY.

A BIT O' THE BARLEY,

MOONEY.

IT'S SIMPLE ENOUGH TO DO

O'MALLEY.

SOME COOLIN', SOME HEATIN'

MOONEY.

AND YOU"LL BE COMPLETIN'

ALL.

A BARREL OR TWO OF BREW!

MOONEY.

YOU CAN CALL IT A LAGER,

O'MALLEY.

AN ALE OR A PORTER

O'LEARY.

A STOUT

CASSIDY.

OR A LIGHT OR A DARK –

O'MALLEY.

IT'S THE VERY BEST THING THAT HAS HAPPENED TO WATER
SINCE NOAH FLOATED HIS ARK!

ALL FOUR.
>OH, A HANDFUL O' HOPS,
>A MEASURE O' MALT
>AND THOUGH FANCIER FOLK MAY SNEER,
>THEY'LL NEVER BE KNOWIN'
>THE RAPTURE OF BLOWIN'
>THE FOAM FROM A PAIL OF BEER!

(MRS. McHUGH comes racing in, all dressed, but a mess.)

McHUGH. Don't you put that away without offerin' me a sip!

MOONEY. Well, she's finally here, she is, the Queen of Canal Street.

McHUGH. Not a word! Never mind the manners, I'll have a sip from your own glass, it's been that topsy turvy a day.

MOONEY. Have a drink. And may your problems be as few and as far between as me dear mother's teeth.

(McHUGH takes a big swig.)

McHUGH. Thanks! *(She drinks.)* Ahhhhh...
>A HANDFUL O' HOPS,
>A BIT O' THE BARLEY
>CAN ANSWER A MAIDEN'S PRAYER!

O'LEARY.
>BEFORE A BAR'S CLOSIN'
>FINE LADS ARE PROPOSIN'
>WHILE LYIN' BENEATH A CHAIR!

O'MALLEY.
>MY HUSBAND O'MALLEY
>HAS GOT HIM A FACE
>THAT COULD STOP ANY CLOCK, IT COULD –
>A HANDFUL O' HOPS
>AND A BIT O' THE BARLEY
>AND EVEN O'MALLEY LOOKS GOOD!

McHUGH.

MY DEAR GRANDMOTHER KATIE WAS BORN ALMOST DEAD
BUT THEY MANAGED TO KEEP HER ALIVE –
THEY JUST WEANED HER ON BEER AND SHE DIED IN HER BED
AT A THIRSTY HUNDRED AND FIVE!

ALL.

OH, A HANDFUL O'HOPS,
A MEASURE O' MALT
AND WE'VE GOT US A CUP O' CHEER!

MOONEY.

WE CAME THROUGH A FAMINE
AND KEPT UP OUR STAMINA –

McHUGH.

GOT US A NOTION
FOR CROSSING AN OCEAN –

ALL.

AND NOW WE ARE SHARIN'
A TOAST TO OLD ERIN
IN PAILS OF BEER !

(The **LADIES** *have become more and more inebriated, laughing and dancing together as they drink.* **DICK** *enters with* **FOSWELL.** **MOONEY** *interrupts the dancing when she sees them…)*

MOONEY. Good! You're together again.

FOSWELL. We've been all over Union Square.

DICK. In and out, up and down, knocking on doors.

FOSWELL. The police don't have a clue.

DICK. And no one's seen Rob.

MOONEY. Well then, you've done all you can. Now no more mopin'. That does no good. In my family when you're down, you dance.

DICK. Mrs. Mooney, I don't feel like –

MOONEY. *(taking* **DICK***'s arm)* There's a fine lad. Now just follow me.

(The dance picks up where it left off as **MOONEY** *and the reluctant* **DICK** *do a few steps.)*

MOONEY. *(cont.)*

> OH YOUR BRAINS'LL GET SMARTER
> YOUR BODY KEEP GROWIN'
> YOU'LL NEVER BE SCRAWNY OR SMALL –

*(**DICK** is spun towards **McHUGH**.)*

McHUGH.

> AS A MATTER OF FACT
> IF THE BEER KEEPS ON FLOWIN'

ALL.

> YOU WON'T NEED VITTLES AT ALL.

*(As the tempo quickens, everyone, including **FOSWELL**, joins in the dancing, swirling together. Exhausted, they all collapse on the stoop.)*

> OH, A HANDFUL O' HOPS,
> A BIT O' THE BARLEY
> AND LIFE'S EVEN LOVELY HERE!
> OUR PROBLEMS ARE SOLVED
> AND OUR TROUBLES DISSOLVED
>
> AS WE SIT ON THE STOOP
> THIS CONGENIAL GROUP
> CAN FORGET ALL OUR WOES
> AS WE BURY OUR NOSE
> IN A PAIL OF BEER!

*(After the number, **McHUGH** begins mopping her brow with her new colored handkerchief. **DICK** sees it.)*

DICK. Lady! Where'd you get that handkerchief?!!

(As she explains, music of "Find That Boy" in…)

McHUGH. One of me boarders has a sick little nephew she keeps locked up in that room. It was his. She gave it to me.

*(**DICK** rushes to grab it)*

Yes, take it! I don't want trouble. It may be cursed.

DICK. No, it's blessed! What's your name?

McHUGH. McNally…McNeil…

THE OTHER LADIES. McHugh!

McHUGH. Mary McHugh – that's me!

DICK. Oh, Mary McHugh! Now think very clearly. Where do you live?

McHUGH. Oh, that I know. 75 Canal Street. See, I knew that!

DICK. Foswell, quick, follow me!

MOONEY. It's a miracle. And the dancin' did it!

(**McHUGH** *swoons. Music up and* **THE BOYS** *run off.*)

Scene Six

(SETTING: **STACIA-JANE** *and* **GERRISH**'s *room.)*

(TIME: Immediately following.)

(AT RISE: **ROB** *is standing center, dressed in the outfit he wore in Union Square.* **STACIA** *is buttoning his jacket.)*

ROB. I'm scared. What if he sees us?

STACIA. He's all the way uptown. I'm going to take you to the police. They'll arrange to get you home.

ROB. What about you? The coppers will get you.

STACIA. I'll leave you at the corner. Just tell them you escaped. I'll get away where he won't find me.

ROB. You don't have to do that. My father will help you.

STACIA. I don't think your father would be very understanding. Let's go.

(She puts on her shawl. She and **ROB** *cross to the door. She opens it.* **GERRISH** *stands in the doorway.)*

GERRISH. And what's this?!

(He enters and closes the door.)

STACIA. I'm just taking the boy out for a little walk. He's not feeling well.

GERRISH. Didn't expect me back so soon, eh? I forgot the kid's ring to put in the letter.

STACIA. Luke, I swear to you, I wasn't –

GERRISH. Ah, Stacia, you make things so difficult.

(He smacks **STACIA** *hard across the face. She falls to the floor.)*

ROB. Stop that!

(He rushes to **GERRISH***, hitting him.)*

GERRISH. We're leaving her behind.

ROB. You shouldn't have hit her! Let me go. Let me go!

(The doorknob turns slowly. **GERRISH** *notices it. He moves with* **ROB** *quickly to behind the door, covering his*

mouth with his hand. The door opens slowly. It's **DICK**. *He sees* **STACIA** *on the floor. He enters and crosses to her.* **GERRISH** *starts to close the door. When he sees it's* **DICK**, *he slams it. He's holding the gun to* **ROB**'s *head.*)

DICK. Gerrish!

GERRISH. Well, Dick! So you're with me. I have the kid. He's our passport outta here.

DICK. It's over.

GERRISH. No! Didn't you listen? It's $50,000! It's the future for both of us.

DICK. There is no future for us. The police are on their way. Give me the gun – give it to me.

(**DICK** *moves towards* **GERRISH**. **ROB** *pulls away and runs toward* **DICK**.)

GERRISH. No!

ROB. Dick, watch out!

DICK. Rob!

(**ROB** *runs to* **DICK**, *who swings* **ROB** *behind him, as* **GERRISH** *fires the gun.* **DICK** *staggers back, falls to the floor.* **GERRISH**, *shaken by what he's done, goes to* **DICK**, *looks at his still body. He turns back to* **ROB**.)

ROB. Dick!

GERRISH. See what your clever friend brought on himself? And you're next if you make a sound. Let's get out of here.

ROB. *(in shock)* I can't go with you.

GERRISH. I said let's move.

ROB. I can't go with you.

GERRISH. I have no time for this.

(*He lays the gun down on the table and, with his back to* **DICK**, *grabs* **ROB**. **DICK** *quietly rises from the floor, moves to the table, picks up the gun, and points it at* **GERRISH**.)

DICK. I don't think so.

(*Startled,* **GERRISH** *turns to him.* **ROB** *runs to him. The door opens and* **OFFICER FOY**, *with gun raised, rushes in.* **FOSWELL** *is right behind him.*)

DICK. This is your kidnapper, Officer Foy. And this boy is Rob Carlisle.

OFFICER FOY. (*handcuffing* **GERRISH**) Who's the woman?

ROB. She was trying to protect me.

OFFICER FOY. She wasn't in on this?

ROB. No. She never was.

DICK. I'll take care of the girl, Officer.

(*He helps the recovering* **STACIA** *to the bed, where she sits.*)

OFFICER FOY. (*to* **DICK**) Isn't this better than a show at the Old Bowery?

GERRISH. (*to* **DICK**) You know what you are? You're lucky. I never was.

(**OFFICER** *exits with* **GERRISH**.)

ROB. How did you do it?

DICK. It all turned on this.

(*pulls out his handkerchief*)

ROB. I mean – Gerrish shot you!

STACIA. He shot you??!!

FOSWELL. He did?!

DICK. Uh-huh.

ROB. But the bullet! Where's the bullet??!!

DICK. Oh, that.

(*opening his jacket*)

It was stopped by my Wall Street prospectuses.

FOSWELL. What??!

(**DICK** *pulls out the contents of his breast pocket, the thick packet of prospectuses, which has a hole through its center.*)

DICK. Yes, Folks. I was saved by good old American Free Enterprise!

Scene Seven

(SETTING: On the trolley.)

(TIME: The next day.)

(AT RISE: A tight GROUP of people, bouncing along, some hanging on to overhead straps, as if on a moving trolley car. Several behind are holding up newspapers. TWO OTHER MEN in front are also reading newspapers. Each lowers his paper as he speaks, revealing who he is...)

CHAPIN. I can't believe it!

HIGGINS. Richard Hunter, a hero, with his name in all the papers.

CHAPIN. And a five thousand dollar reward!

HIGGINS. I am in such pain.

CHAPIN. My little plan sort of backfired, didn't it?

HIGGINS. Oh, yes! We certainly went to town when we smashed up Snobden's precious little rag shop!

(From the rear of the GROUP, one man lowers his paper. It is SNOBDEN. He moves forward, glaring at the employees who, seeing him, are aghast.)

HIGGINS & CHAPIN. Oops!

(They disappear as SNOBDEN puts down his paper and moves forward.)

(segue)

Scene Eight

*(**SETTING**: Heading Uptown)*

*(**TIME**: Seamlesss transition from previous scene. It's several days later and moves back and forth in time.)*

*(**AT RISE**: **SNOBDEN** steps from the previous scene into this one. He is elegantly dressed, and donning an expensive hat.)*

FIRST MAN (MAN #3). Very Snappy, Snobden.

SECOND MAN (MAN #1). What's the occasion?

Song - *NORTH OF FOURTEENTH STREET*

SNOBDEN.
> I AM IN THE VERY BEST HAT
> THAT'S SOLD TO GENTS OF TASTE AND REKNOWN –
> YOU MUST BE DRESSED
> IN THE VERY, VERY BEST
> WHEN YOU'RE GOING TO A PARTY UPTOWN!

MEN (MAN #1, MAN #3).
> YOU'RE GOING TO A PARTY UPTOWN, UPTOWN

SNOBDEN.
> A RESPECTABLE PARTY UPTOWN!

ALL.
> WHEN TRAVELLING NORTH OF FOURTEENTH STREET
> ONE HAS TO KEEP UP WITH THE REST –

SNOBDEN.
> I'M READY FOR NORTH OF FOURTEENTH STREET
> FROM TOP TO BOTTOM IN SNOBDEN'S BEST!

*(**MRS. MOONEY** enters with **MRS. McHUGH**.)*

Ah, Mrs. Mooney. You're going to Allen Carlisle's party I see.

MOONEY. I am indeed Mr. Snobden. With my friend Mary McHugh.

McHUGH. How do.

SNOBDEN. *(He tips his hat to her.)* And where is Mr. Mooney, may I ask?

MOONEY. Oh he's been missing these eight years.

SNOBDEN. Eight years!

MOONEY. I know. Under the law, I am a widow.

SNOBDEN. Isn't life a kick in the pants?

MOONEY. I couldn't have said it better.

(He tips his hat, a happy man.)

McHUGH. *(interrupting)*
I'M IN HER BEST SECOND-HAND HAT

MOONEY.
AND I'M IN HER BEST HAND-ME-DOWN GOWN

BOTH.
WE BOTH ARE DRESSED
IN EACH OTHER'S SECOND BEST
FOR WE'RE GOING TO A PARTY UPTOWN!

WE'RE GOING TO A PARTY UPTOWN, UPTOWN

MOONEY.
A PROTESTANT PARTY UPTOWN!

Come on, dearie. We don't want to be late for the free food.

McHUGH. And the beer, dear. There's bound to be beer.

MOONEY. I dunno. We may get stuck with champagne.

(MOONEY and SNOBDEN are arm in arm, McHUGH following. As they exit, FOSWELL appears, adjusting an ill-fitting suit.)

FOSWELL.
NEVER GO TO PARTIES –
NEVER SAW THE NEED –
I HOPE THAT MISTER CARLISLE
HAS SOMETHING GOOD TO READ!

SNOBDEN. *(returning)* Good to see you, Foswell. Before we go in, I wanted to tell you that Hunter's agreed to return to work as the replacement for my ex-chief clerk.

FOSWELL. He told me.

SNOBDEN. He made one proviso though.

FOSWELL. Oh? That he didn't tell me.

SNOBDEN. He insisted I try to convince you to be my new office boy.

FOSWELL. He did?

SNOBDEN. His exact words were, "I don't mean to sound presumptuous, but I'd like you to employ Henry Foswell, because he's bright and full of finesse."

FOSWELL. *(to himself)* He found a home for them!

SNOBDEN. So what do you say? Will Foswell and Hunter join Silas Snobden, Inc.?

FOSWELL. Hunter and Foswell will. Yes!

SNOBDEN. Excellent!

(They exit together. **HIGGINS** *and* **CHAPIN** *enter, crossing in the other direction, each carrying a shoeshine box.)*

HIGGINS. *(to* **CHAPIN***)*

THAT PLAN OR YOURS HAS GOT US BOTH FIRED!
I'LL NEVER FIND A JOB IN THIS TOWN –
AND WHAT'S WORSE YET,
CAUSE OF YOU I'LL NEVER GET
TO THAT ELEGANT PARTY UPTOWN!

I'M MISSING THAT PARTY UPTOWN, UPTOWN
THAT FANCY-PANTS PARTY UPTOWN!

I NEVER GET NORTH OF FOURTEENTH STREET –
I REALLY WANTED TO GO!

CHAPIN.

I'LL KICK YOU SO NORTH OF FOURTEENTH STREET
THAT YOUR FAT REAR END'LL BE FILLED WITH SNOW!

(As they continue to argue, **MICKEY** *suddenly appears.)*

MICKEY. Hey! You two! Outta here! This is my territory!

(As **MICKEY** *chases a terrified* **HIGGINS** *and* **CHAPIN** *off,* **STACIA** *enters, wearing a beautiful dress and hat.)*

STACIA.
> I AM IN MY VERY FIRST HAT –
> IT GOES WITH THIS, MY VERY FIRST GOWN –
> TODAY'S THE DAY,
> LIKE A LADY IN A PLAY,
> I AM GOING TO A PARTY UP –

(**CARLISLE** *has entered, interrupts.*)

CARLISLE. Miss Hauser, will you do me the honor?

STACIA. You continue to rescue me.

CARLISLE. I think it's the other way round. Would you allow me to escort you in to dinner?

STACIA. I'd like that. Thank you!

CARLISLE. You see? Things have a way of working out.
> YOU'RE GOING TO A PARTY UPTOWN, UPTOWN –

STACIA.
> MY VERY FIRST PARTY UPTOWN!
>
> I NEVER THOUGHT NORTH OF FOURTEENTH STREET
> COULD EVER BE PART OF MY DREAM –
> BUT SUDDENLY NORTH OF FOURTEENTH STREET
> IS NOT AS FAR AS IT USED TO SEEM!

(**CARLISLE** *takes her arm, and they leave together.* **DICK** *appears, resplendent in the suit he'd first admired in* **SNOBDEN**'s *window, with the fancy handkerchief prominently displayed in the pocket. We are now, at last, in* **CARLISLE**'s *elegant drawing room.* **FOSWELL** *appears, holding a bootblack box.*)

FOSWELL. Look at you. You are a gentleman.

DICK. (*He sees the box.*) What's that?

FOSWELL. I found this in the library.

DICK. (*He takes it and reads from a plaque on it.*) "Allen Carlisle, Bootblack."

FOSWELL. Can you imagine??

DICK. "I knew a kid once who only got three cents a shine," he said. That kid was him.

FOSWELL. No more king of the bootblacks for you. They can't call you that anymore. Now it's "Richard Hunter, Esquire."

DICK. That's right. A young gentleman on his way to fame and fortune.

ALL. *(gradually appearing)*
WE'RE GOING TO A PARTY UPTOWN UPTOWN!
WE'RE GOING TO A PARTY UPTOWN UPTOWN!
A GLORIOUS PARTY UPTOWN!

DICK.
I'M FINALLY NORTH OF FOURTEENTH STREET
THAT THOROUGHBRED SECTION OF TOWN!

ALL.
AND NOW THAT WE'RE NORTH OF FOURTEENTH STREET
WE THINK WE NEVER MAY GO BACK DOWN.

(curtain)

Finale & Bows

(The bows are taken, first the ensemble, then the principals in ones and twos, bowing to upbeat music varied. **DICK** *takes final solo bow and as he enters, the music changes to "Yes!" ...)*

(When **DICK** *has completed his bow, he sings:)*

DICK.

WILL IT ALL TURN OUT ALL RIGHT?
THAT'S ANYBODY'S GUESS –
TRYING ONCE AGAIN MAY LEAD
TO FAILURE OR SUCCESS –

(perhaps spoken)

COULD I MAKE THE WHITE HOUSE
MY NEW FORWARDING ADDRESS?

FULL COMPANY.

YES!
YES!
YES!

(final curtain)

Other plays by the authors of
Shine!

Paris is Out!
A Comedy by Richard Seff

The Whole Ninth Floor
A Comedy by Richard Seff

Abe
A Musical by Roger Dean Anderson
and Lee Goldsmith

Please visit our website **samuelfrench.com** for complete descriptions and licensing information.

OTHER TITLES AVAILABLE FROM SAMUEL FRENCH

PARIS IS OUT!

Richard Seff

Comedy / 3m, 5f / 2 Interiors

Hortense and Daniel, a married couple of over 40 years, plan to embark on their first European vacation, but the two have very different outlooks on travel. Daniel is convinced he will be unimpressed by the other side of the pond. His conditions for the trip are: no Paris, no Venice, no shopping, sightseeing, or speaking in French. Hortense, on the other hand, is full of life and eager to experience Europe fully. When Daniel embarrasses Hortense in front of family and friends, she announces that the trip is cancelled. As her adult children try to convince her to forgive Daniel, Hortense must decide how she feels about the man with whom she has shared a life for 40 years. Daniel, in turn, to save his marriage must show how much he appreciates Hortense.

Paris is Out! is a witty and heart-warming comedy about the triumphs and struggles of a lifelong marriage.

> "The audience gave every evidence of loving it!"
> – *The New York Times*

> "The audience around me was laughing hysterically."
> – ABC TV

SAMUELFRENCH.COM

OTHER TITLES AVAILABLE FROM SAMUEL FRENCH

THE WHOLE NINTH FLOOR

Richard Seff

Comedy / 6m, 5f / Interior

Across the street from the 'mad men' of Madison Avenue live the Ten Percenters of the National Talent Agency. It's the same time, 1962, a secretary is still a toy, boys will still be boys, but the times they are a changin'. Audiences will love to hear what's happening on *The Whole Ninth Floor.*

"First impression is that it is a string of jokes tied together rather loosely. A moment's concentration brings home however the basic fact that Seff weaves a story based on the young man's intense and insistent desire to do the right thing. The laughs come fast, and they are plentiful."
– *The Patterson Call*

"The comedy construction of *The Whole Ninth Floor* is made up of wall-to-wall witticisms. Seff has a good ear and facile pen for manufacturing witty dialog. Also he obviously knows, from first hand experience, Madison Avenue and the talent agency area of show business, for his prototypes and inside trade references are accurate and appropriate."
– *The Scotch Plain Times*

"A sparkling new comedy, a tremendously funny play."
– *The Herald News*

SAMUELFRENCH.COM

OTHER TITLES AVAILABLE FROM SAMUEL FRENCH

ABE

Book and Lyrics by Lee Goldsmith
Music by Roger Anderson

Musical / 16m, 9f

"The founding fathers got their own musical with *1776*,
so why not *Abe?*"
– *Playbill.com*

Abe is a new musical about the early life of Abraham Lincoln. The show explores his youth as a flatboat pilot on the Mississippi, his early love for Ann Rutledge, his troubled marriage to the difficult and mentally fragile Mary Todd, and his attempt to be a good father to his sons. The story follows Abe from his earliest attempts at self-improvement through the 1860 election which made him the 16th president of an already fracturing United States.

The score is fully orchestrated and uses bold, melodic and traditional musical theatre styles that embrace the story's period and Americana roots. It can be produced fully staged or as a concert performance. The musical features a large cast and requires strong singers: baritone, soprano, mezzo-soprano, 3 adult male singing roles, 3 male children singing roles, male/female chorus with many speaking roles.

SAMUELFRENCH.COM

OTHER TITLES AVAILABLE FROM SAMUEL FRENCH

AMERICAN TALES

Book and Lyrics by Ken Stone
Music by Jan Powell

Musical in two acts, based on stories
by classic American writers

Musical in two acts, based on stories by classic American writers / 4m, 1f / Period costumes and set pieces, mid to late 19th century

**Ovation Award nomination for Best Book/Lyrics/Music
Kleban Award winner, Libretto** *(Bartleby, the Scrivener)*

Act I, *The Loves of Alonzo Fitz Clarence and Rosannah Ethelton*, is from Mark Twain's story of two people falling in love at a great distance with the aid of that brand-new invention, the telephone. Alonzo in Maine and Rosannah in California meet by the accident of crossed wires and each falls in love with an imagined ideal of the other. So complete is their self-deception that even when brought face to face they cannot recognize each other. Love is found, lost, and found again. Played as period melodrama, but the relevance to 21st century dating habits is clear.

Act II, *Bartleby, the Scrivener*, is dramatized from Herman Melville's slyly funny but ultimately tragic story. Building on the theme of human connections made and missed, this act takes a darker turn, looking at people who occupy the closest of quarters and yet don't really communicate at all. Bartleby, employed as a copyist in a law office of the 1840s, inexplicably begins to refuse to work, forcing his colleagues to ask themselves the transforming question that ends the play: What do we owe to the people who come into our lives?

"Excellent new musical."
– Critic's Choice, *The Los Angeles Times*

SAMUELFRENCH.COM

OTHER TITLES AVAILABLE FROM SAMUEL FRENCH

A TALE OF TWO CITIES, THE MUSICAL

Book, Music and Lyrics by Jill Santoriello

Musical / 7m, 3f, 1f child, Ensemble (doubling possible)

Outer Critics Circle Award Nominee - Outstanding New Broadway Musical

Two men in love with the same woman. Two cities swept up in revolution. One last chance for a man to redeem his wasted life and change the world. Based on Charles Dickens' masterpiece, *A Tale of Two Cities* is a musical that focuses on the love triangle between young beauty Lucie Manette, French aristocrat Charles Darnay and drunken English cynic Sydney Carton - all caught in the clutches of the bloody French Revolution.

Fresh off its Broadway run, *A Tale of Two Cities* is the perfect addition to any theatre's season! Appropriate for all ages and audiences, this classic story of love, revolution, and redemption is what the *Associated Press* called, "the return to the era of big blockbusters such as *Les Miserables*, *Phantom*, and *Miss Saigon*."

"A Broadway must see! Everything is here to stir the soul—young love, purity, vengeance, villainy, valor—all played out against that historic revolution."
– *The Connecticut Post*

"It's got a rousing score and the story's noble sacrifice, beautifully realized by Jill Santoriello, doesn't leave a dry eye in the house."
– *HuffingtonPost.com*

"It's epic, electrifying musical theatre at its grandest."
– *TalkEntertainment.com*

SAMUELFRENCH.COM

www.ingramcontent.com/pod-product-compliance
Lightning Source LLC
Chambersburg PA
CBHW070644300426
44111CB00013B/2258